BEING HUMAN

Travels with Stanley

Angelica Sorel

Sorel Press

For my ọmọ rẹrẹ, Kate and Jake.

ANGELICA SOREL

Ẹ KAABỌ

The plane was crowded. I'd stood in line at Heathrow Airport with Nigerian travellers trundling the hugest suitcases I'd ever seen, and those large checkered zip-top bags made of woven plastic nicknamed "Ghana must go".[1]

Once on board, I slipped into the toilet to change into a bright blue hand-printed cotton loose top and wrap around skirt worn by many Nigerian women, the *buba* and wrapper I'd had made on my first visit to the country a year before. By the time we arrived in Lagos, I was ready.

As I disembarked and walked through the airport, I was met with approving smiles.

"*Ẹ kaabọ*" beamed the immigration official, "welcome."

"*Iyawo!*" men called as I passed, greeting me with the word for a new wife.

The protective swathe of my outfit worked its magic. Stitched into its seams were $100 dollar bills. Musing on how to transport enough money to support myself for a year, I'd struck on the idea of turning my clothes into a walking bank. I sauntered past the throng of customs officials, immigration officers and touts with several thousand dollars crisp in the hem of my skirt, remembering my instructions: don't give anyone your passport, don't give anyone money, don't trust anyone with your bags.

Making my way through the crowded arrivals hall, I greeted the blast of warm, humid air and the hubbub of the airport's throng of touts that welcomed me to Nigeria with a broad smile.

I'd arrived.

There's a Nigeria that exists in the cautionary tales of those white people who arrive in the country to make money, save souls, or perform acts of rescue in the name of Development. Many live in closely guarded quarters in the plusher areas of Lagos. The more adventurous amongst them venture onto the mainland, leaving behind the well-groomed lawns of Victoria Island or Ikoyi for the shouts of hawkers wending their way between vehicles jammed in Lagos' notorious go-slows.

Not for them the sticky warmth of the city. Their drivers were there to ensure that they never need to sully their feet by walking or expose themselves to the harshness of the Nigerian sun. They are whisked to their offices, their clubs and to the commissary or delicatessen to buy with their generous hardship allowances the foods that remind them of home. Theirs is a world regulated by air-conditioning. With their thermostats dialling down the tropics and a fridge stocked with imported familiarity, the only trace of Nigeria in their homes is the kind of African carving that graces many an expatriate home.

In the small towns that spread into the interior, white people are a rare sight. Only the missionaries - and the occasional anthropologist - venture off the highways.

Of course, I had no idea of any of this when I arrived. I was not at all interested in white people or their protected existences. As for me, well, white as I was too, I held the development industry in contempt and reserved the greatest of all scorn for evangelical missionaries indulging their white saviour complex.

Being white had allowed me an unfair share of adventures. I'd hitchhiked my way through Central Africa, crossing the Zaire-

Uganda border with a diamond smuggler who plied me with altar wine from a goatskin flask, supplied by the local bishop. I'd survived hair-raising bus rides through the Andes, a sojourn in the red-light district of a Brazilian coastal city, and nights out clubbing in downtown Caracas, Lima and La Paz. I'd even once thumbed a ride from an armed convoy vehicle riddled with bullet holes and sped down the Beira Corridor between Zimbabwe and the Mozambican coast in the middle of the civil war, driven by an impulsive desire to see the sea.

I came out of all this with disdain for the ragbag of youth who rolled from one destination to another comparing prices, haggling for pennies and partying. I'd been one of them myself. But I was now something entirely different.

I was an Anthropologist in search of a Fieldsite.

GOING TO THE FIELD

For the would-be anthropologist, Going to The Field is a defining experience. One minute you're an ordinary person, curious about why humans do what they do. The next you Go to The Field and you come back from it an Anthropologist. Part of the mystique of this rite de passage is that it is never made entirely clear what *actually happens* when you do fieldwork. It is a secret shared only by initiates. They may trade some of their own stories with their students as cautionary tales. But most fully-fledged anthropologists keep it pretty close to their chests. It's like talking about what childbirth is really like to women pregnant with their first child: you just don't tell them too much of the details.

When I began studying for my PhD at SOAS, London University's School of Oriental and African Studies, I knew that I would sooner or later be destined to Go to The Field. Quite where or what my field would be, I was made to understand, was completely up to me. Anthropologists studied everything. You could be a specialist in the magical medicines of a recently discovered Amazon tribe, Balinese cock fights, English queuing habits and weather talk, Jamaican dance hall romances or Japanese dining rituals. The world was my oyster. White privilege and my British passport insulated me against anything as burdensome as thinking politically about imposing myself on a People for the purpose of studying them.

All I had to do was come up with a suitable topic.

My excursions in the library took me around the globe and back again. And then one day, I found a book wedged between a collection of older volumes encased in dull worn cloth. It had a glossy black cover with script the colour of fresh blood. On it was an African mask, a figure of a woman with enormous eyes wearing an impassive expression. It was called *Gelede: Art and Female Power Among the Yoruba*. I became obsessed with this book. I'd take it out of the library, take it back, take it out again. I wrote to the authors asking them some of the many questions exploding in my imagination. Busy and important American academics, they didn't reply.

I was mesmerised by the idea of a religion that celebrated women's economic and sexual autonomy, one in which women were believed to have such power that they were feared by men. It was so far removed from what I knew as religion.

My village Anglican church primary school upbringing in rural northern England in the 1970s had a prophylactic effect on me, putting me off organised religion for life. My teacher, the vicar's wife, was a stocky woman in her late 50s fond of wielding her umbrella as a precaution against any misbehaviour. "I'll heeet you now!" she'd declare in a loud voice, narrowing her eyes and glaring at you until you'd squirmed enough for her liking. She had a sadistic bent. If she saw that you liked something, she'd make sure you didn't get it. Like being able to pick between making chickadees for the church fete or knitting dishcloths out of dirty grey coloured string. I always got the dishcloths. I'd have to content myself with stealing glimpses of more favoured classmates sewing together pieces of yellow fake fur with orange felt beaks and little plastic eyes with bits in them that rolled around.

The services we were forced to attend twice a week in the dank, musty-smelling, village church were strange at first, and then mind-numbingly boring. All that getting up, sitting down, kneeling and muttering. I'd pretend to mutter too and when there were those long prayers that everyone seemed to know by heart, I'd peer around me to see if I could catch sight of another person who didn't have their eyes shut.

Through a child's eyes, the things Christians believed in seemed to be really strange. Turning water into wine. Feeding hundreds of people with a couple of fish. And that was the small stuff. The church had a gory looking statue of Jesus on the cross and I remember spending hours puzzling over the idea that someone could return from the dead after being nailed to a piece of wood and bleeding to death. The statue had big nails and red marks, but there wasn't any blood. If someone was going to die from losing blood, surely it would be spurting out, I reasoned. When I'd hurt myself climbing trees, so much blood had poured out of my leg that when I ran indoors my mum wrapped a towel around it and pressed hard until the sticky red liquid stopped flowing. These details were important to me. I wanted to be a doctor when I grew up.

When I was seven years old, I was found out for the terrible truth that I was not a Christian. I went home weeping. "My teacher told me I didn't have a name and I will go to hell when I die", I sobbed. My father was up in arms, threatening to go to the school to demand that I was removed from anything to do with religious instruction and that the teacher was chastised for bullying me. A die-hard atheist, he'd been inoculated by a brush with the Church of England that had lasted until he studied philosophy. He'd got to the Big Questions, and wondered to himself, *how do people believe all this?*

I was mortified. "Please, please don't do that," I begged.

I just wanted to be normal. I was already strange for having a foreign mum, a secret I hid as closely as I could. And now this.

In the end, he let it go and got his own back on the vicar's wife by introducing me to the idea of religion as the opium of the people, explaining that people's minds get addled by believing in things that aren't true, and that it was so they can be controlled more easily. He also refused to attend the church fete, where the chickadees and dishcloths we'd produced were sold to raise money for the church.

Gelede: Art and Female Power Among the Yoruba offered me an entirely different kind of religion. Here, in this lavishly produced volume, full of black and white photos of masquerade performances in rural Nigeria, I read about the power of the feminine. The book took its name from the masked dance ritual itself: *Gelede.* The masks were carved in honour of "our mothers", *awon iya* in the Yoruba language. *Awon iya,* mothers and witches, symbolised the elemental force that is life itself. The masquerade came out to celebrate the many sides of women's power, fearsome and mighty: the power to give birth and the power to take life, through witchcraft.

Intrigued, I began reading my way through books and articles about Yoruba religion. I encountered a glorious panoply of deities, *orisas.* Many were associated with natural forces – the sea, fire, water, wind. I could relate to a material and felt world shaped through their powers. The goddess Oya found a special place in my imagination. Known as Iansã in Brazil, Oya - whose colour is red and whose day is Wednesday - has a disruptive, restless energy that makes things happen. Oya, who didn't want to marry, or settle, or be domesticated. Oya, the fiery spirit that resists, rebels, and animates change.

My own spirit had until then lacked any conception of spirituality. All of this drew me with an excitement that I came to understand as the spark of the would-be anthropologist. I was intensely curious to know more. I learnt how the religion had spread and evolved over the centures as the African diaspora, dislocated from the continent by the Atlantic slave trade, created memories, rituals and stories. Anthropologists had played their part, publishing books that became used to reconstruct and reorient religious beliefs and practices in the diaspora.

I read of how shrines of the *orisas* had been desecrated by loutish Christian youth in the 1950s, members of a witch-finding movement called *atinga* that swept through western Nigeria. The shrines were never to be rebuilt. Neglected gods expired, robbed of their followers by the brash new religions and their promises of salvation and redemption. Those who knew how to perform the rituals had mostly died. I heard of how those holding onto the vestiges of the old beliefs were now sending their children to Brazil to learn from the descendants of slaves seized from Yoruba sub-ethnic groups and trafficked along land corridors to the coast.

I also learnt that Yoruba masquerades, including *Gelede*, were still performed in towns across the southwest of Nigeria and over the border into Benin, in and around the old kingdom of Ketu. The masks used in these performances were imbued with the power of magical medicine and of witchcraft.

I became determined to go to Nigeria. I bought my own copy of the book. I'd turn the black glossy cover and peer inside it, combing its pages for ideas. Out of it grew a research project. It was a strange hybrid, bridging my fascination with the power of the mothers and my curiosity with what I came to recognise as quasi-colonial concerns with the health and wellbeing of the people living in those small towns, in a region with poor health services, endemic malaria and a band of infertility that took so many women from healer to prophet to quack in search of a child. Shockingly high maternal mortality rates meant that numbers of those women found through pregnancy not life, but death. I saw in *Gelede* the potential for a health promotion project that could help preserve women's fertility and their lives.

Full of zeal for my idea, I won a grant. The grant took me to Nigeria. And that was how I ended up one day on a rattling old brown and yellow Nissan passenger van that the locals called *danfo*, speeding towards the Benin border to attend my first *Gelede* performance.

IN PRAISE OF
THOSE WHO PAY

I'd set off from Ibadan wearing the *buba* and wrapper I'd worn to enter the country. Lacking anywhere else to keep my money, I still had the dollar bills sewn into its seams. They made for a slightly starched looking side panel, malleable enough not to give my secret away.

For the last few weeks, I'd been making forays into the south-west of the country, in search of a place where I could study *Gelede*. Amongst the range of reactions when I announced that I'd come from England to study *Gelede*, I'd encountered smirks, bemusement, straight out laughter, patient explanation that in this Nigeria the only people who believed in this kind of thing were old and uneducated people, and a large dose of generous indulgence in what was clearly some kind of English eccentricity.

Undeterred, I'd focused on the westernmost edge of the southern part of the country, the area bordering the Benin Republic. Using *danfos* and shared taxis, I wandered around the border towns strung along the straight line which colonial officials had drawn on a map in Paris shortly before the end of the previous century, as Britain and France marked up their claims to what would become their colonial dominions.

I soon ended up arousing the suspicions of Nigerian border

officials.

One of the immigration officers began following me after he'd hauled me off a crowded *danfo* heading for the border. He demanded my passport, then waved it at me, menacing me with the threat that if I so much as stepped across the invisible line dividing Nigeria from Benin, he would seize it. I faced an awkward moment in the house of the king of one of these towns, as I paid my respects. "Come closer," he commanded from a dark wooden throne with elaborately carved arm rests at the end of a long, narrow room with a shiny concrete floor. I would willingly have paid my respects in closer proximity. That is, if it had not been pointed out to me by the immigration official, who had followed me to its door, that I'd have been crossing the border without a re-entry permit.

I could swear the official was lurking outside, peering in through the slatted glass window. Keeping tabs on me as well he might, I reflected, given the treatment of Nigerian visitors to the UK.

"Your Highness," I stuttered, "I must remain here, as I only have a visa for Nigeria and no permit to cross the border." I genuflected in situ and fled.

In one of these towns, I'd found the most promising lead so far.

"*Gelede?*" asked a young man I'd asked for directions and who'd plied me with his curiosity. "Yes, we do that here. When do you want to see it?"

I hadn't anticipated the possibility of a command performance.

Some hours later, another young man arrived with a drum tucked under his arm, with a taut goatskin head and rope straps criss-crossing its body. He took a thin curved stick that looked a bit like the spindly handle of an umbrella and squeezed the drum with his elbow as he tapped out the lines that I assumed to be a string of praises. I was impressed. The first youth had returned with a large wooden mask carved with the figure of a woman with a large bird on her head. I recognised the symbolism of the bird, associating women with the power of witchcraft.

I felt like I was being a real anthropologist, at last!

"Madam, where camera?"

The young man with the drum had stopped. The two of them were looking at me expectantly.

"I don't have a camera"

"How are you going to make your film, Madam?"

It transpired that some Americans had been in the area a couple of years ago, paying good money for people to perform *Gelede*. For the two lads, another white person rocking up in the same place meant a film, and abundant wads of Naira.

No camera. No wads of Naira. I was a pretty useless prospect. They quickly became bored with me. They made their excuses and were gone.

I sought directions to the palace and found the king sitting on a dais in a narrow mint green room with a shiny concrete floor. He smiled kindly and with an air of indulgence, told me that I should stay in his house for the night and then he would send me with his driver to the next town.

A room was made ready for me. As dusk fell a large bowl of hot water was brought to me to bathe, and then a delicious dinner of rice and a stew fragrant with palm oil and pepper arrived on a tray. The next day, I was brought toast, that most English of foods, made with spongey white sliced bread. And then it was time for me to take my leave and move on to the next town. I went to pay my respects and give my thanks.

This gracious generosity was my experience of Nigeria. I have never in my life encountered such kindness and such care. And that has stayed with me, in how I treat others. In studying what it meant to be human, becoming the anthropologist I am now, Nigeria shaped me as a human being. This expansive, populous country has its share of bad eggs, that was for sure. But as I travelled around in search of a fieldsite, I met only goodness. And being open to that goodness brought me experiences I might otherwise never have had.

I returned to Ibadan and within a few days I was back on the road again. I'd been tipped off by an academic in Ibadan about a possible performance of *Gelede* that very weekend. The place was far, further up on the Benin border. I hoped that it was far enough out of the beat of my nemesis the immigration official.

As the *danfo* tore its way into the hinterlands west of Ibadan, I became increasingly aware of what a pain it was for my fellow passengers to be in my company. Travelling by public transport seemed to weaken the magic of my *buba* and wrapper. Border officials and police would spy my white face through the window of the *danfo* and step into the road to halt the vehicle. Then they'd haul me out to grill me, hoping all the time that I'd dip into my purse to 'settle' the matter. It wasn't only that hadn't yet developed the right way of giving a bribe. It was that I saw it as the thin end of the wedge: once I started dishing out bribes, it would be difficult to travel anywhere in the area without being stopped to pay a 'toll'. I steadfastly refused.

This resulted in a catalogue of delays to our journey.

To the amusement and relief of my fellow travellers, I developed a tactic to make my white skin disappear. I took to lying back in my seat as we approached the checkpoint, as if asleep, with head, face and hands covered with the voluminous indigo cloth of my head-tie. We'd sail past. Even when we were summoned to draw to a halt so the officer could fish for a bribe from the driver, I wasn't spotted. So rare was it for a white woman to be travelling by the form of transport used by most Nigerians, the officials would never have even thought that the sleeping figure swathed in cheap hand-printed cloth might have been worth asking for their papers.

I was almost asleep under my head-tie when the *danfo* came to a stop at our destination. Expecting another checkpoint, I remained as still as a corpse. By then I was bathed in sweat, rivulets racing their way down my body. I began thinking of the dollars, imagining them stained with unsavoury blotches, when I was jabbed gently with the elbow of my neighbour, and felt her press her body against mine. Her impatience was palpable.

"*Oyinbo*, we have arrived-o! You can show your face. Let's move."

I pushed the curtain of cloth aside, shuffled out of the sliding door and took account of the fading light. A deep apricot glow backlit the rusting corrugated iron roofs and terracotta mud plaster houses, neatly arranged along what seemed to be the town's main street. Children drew together in a gaggle to observe the white woman stepping down from the *danfo*, light brown hair dishevelled and sticking in lumps to her head and light blue eyes that marked her out as someone from somewhere very different.

I'd read before leaving Ibadan that the Catholic church had a guest house. These were the days before there was even a phone line to the place. I hitched up my wrapper, running my hand along the crumpled seam to straighten it, and made my way towards the large stone building at the junction ahead, its wooden cross a sign that it might be the place I was looking for. As I neared the church, I heard the sound of singing and the heavy thud of movement, which I soon recognised as the coordinated dance steps of an identically dressed troupe.

"That's beautiful," I said to the young woman who ushered me in through the doorway.

"Yes," she said, "it's *Gelede*".

Inside the church, I saw rows of women dancing in the open

space at the front of the pews. The sight gave me goosebumps. It took me back to the *terreiros* of Salvador, the Afro-Brazilian ritual spaces where I'd spent a summer doing a dissertation project and wrestling with feeling I was a spectator in other people's lives with nothing to contribute except the nuisance of my curiosity: an anthropological voyeur.

A plaster Virgin Mary beamed on the scene with a beatific smile. The women were singing as they danced. I couldn't make out the words, but I kept hearing *Jesu, Jesu*. Jesus. I left the church, puzzled. The American art historians had not written anything about all this. What was going on? What was *Gelede* dance doing in this space, one I associated with a spirituality so alien to a version of female power as fierce and fearsome as that of *awon iya*?

The nuns offered me a room for the night. I put my slim travel bag in the guesthouse before walking into town. The main square was decked out with lights, rows of plastic chairs and a wooden dais. There was a hum of activity, the shrill squeal of small children playing, women bustling around with vats of steaming stews and trays with dozens of pats of the Nigerian equivalent of mashed potato – *fufu* and *eba*, pounded, fermented cassava wrapped in neat pats and clothed in clingfilm – and men greeting their friends and relatives as they arrived to take their seats.

I'd taken a chance on the tip from the academic in Ibadan. It turned out to be right. There was to be a performance that night. As dusk fell, vehicles arrived and discharged people dressed in elaborate lace and the expensive thick cotton fabric I came to know as guinea brocade. It was sold in large bales in London's Petticoat Lane and in markets across coastal West Africa, the cloth of choice of the middle classes. Tailors rustled up flowing robes for men called *agbada*, with a matching cap that was a cross between a beret and a fez. Women wore the cloth as *buba* and wrapper, matched with extravagant head ties made from

17

starched linen, gauze, lace or matching fabric, long lengths of cloth - like the one under which I concealed my whiteness - whirled into veritable confections.

Dusk was settling over the town. Soon it was night. Paraffin lamps strung up around the square were lit, and rows of white plastic chairs rapidly filled with a crowd voluble with excitement. Soon enough, the masquerade began. The troupe of dancers entered the clearing in the middle of the square. They were greeted with a fanfare from talking drums that sang the lyrics and pounded the rhythms for the dance. A large gold Mercedes cruised to a stop. A portly man stepped out, dressed in an immaculate white lace *agbada* with gold piping. He was accompanied by a woman resplendent in gold coloured guinea brocade with the most elaborate head tie I had ever seen. Everyone shushed and pointed and whispered; I turned to my neighbour, the ever-curious anthropologist, and hissed "who is he?". He was, it turned out, a son of the town who had made it big in Lagos.

A procession of dancers burst out from behind one of the houses, with large wooden-carved masks balancing on top of vibrantly coloured cloth flaps, which flounced and bounced as they swirled. The masked dancers filed towards him. Accompanied by a battery of talking drums singing his praises, the dancers fawned and bowed and scraped around him as the audience clapped enthusiastic applause.

As the night wore on, the scene repeated itself with the notaries of the town as the centre of attention. The dancers' masks had all the symbolism of female power. The dance, however, seemed to have become domesticated in the service of patriarchy. I watched with mounting despair. My elaborately crafted project evaporated before my eyes. I could, I reasoned, study how a masquerade celebrating women's elemental powers had come to be co-opted by the Catholic church and turned to celebrating Big Men. But I had not got the stomach or the heart.

I went back to Ibadan reeling with my loss.

I picked up the densely written document that I'd been required to produce to be allowed to progress to fieldwork. Twenty thousand words. Flipping disconsolately through its pages, I began to laugh at myself and at my folly. True, one of my supervisors had seen it coming and had tried to dissuade me. His comments on the document I'd submitted were acerbic. I was indignant. This idea had won me my grant, and I used that as my defence.

As I came to my senses, I realised he'd been right all along. And there I was, stranded, without a project. I didn't even have a passport. I'd had to find a fixer to send it to the capital, Abuja, to regularise my presence as a foreigner. Who knew how many months it would be before its return with the official stamp displaying my residence permit.

Old-fashioned anthropology, I reasoned, was all about just going somewhere, *being there*, listening, tuning into what matters. Taking copious fieldnotes. 'Writing up', the process of weaving it all together, involved telling stories about anything the anthropologist found. Anything.

It was time to get traditional.

FINDING MY PLACE

If anyone had told me before I set off on my fieldwork that I'd end up living in the only town in the whole region where *Gelede* masquerade had never been performed, I'd have scoffed in disbelief. But that's where I ended up.

The first glimpse I had of Ilemi was through the broken window of an old *danfo*, hurtling as fast as it could along the wide tarred road from Badagry. We swung past a brightly painted plaster virgin, prominently placed outside the large Catholic church at the fringes of the town, then plummeted down a steep slope into the luxuriant green of the swampy forest and up along a road densely lined with stores and stalls into the main street. The van came to a sudden halt next to an untidy row of stalls and I was jostled out.

I had not intended to stop at Ilemi. I was on my way to Igbessa, the next stop on my quest for a fieldsite. I didn't reach Igbessa that day or the next.

It was hot. I had travelled to Badagry on one of the huge yellow beasts of a bus called *molue*, seeking respite from the crowds of Lagos. Crammed together on narrow metal seats, my fellow passengers shot me glances of surprise: this, the lowliest form of transport, was hardly the place one would expect to see an *oyinbo*. The bus lurched along, belching smoke and rattling ominously until we reached a crowded motorpark. Dazed by the journey, I was shunted into the waiting *danfo* by a helpful fellow passenger. By the time I reached Ilemi I was crushed, bruised and very thirsty.

The rusty Toyota transporter had disgorged its cramped and shaken passengers by the market. I stumbled into the first stall I could see, in search of a cold Coca Cola. The owner of the stall was immaculately dressed in an outfit of peacock blue lace, studded with sequins. She replied to my halting Yoruba in fluent English, pausing after serving me my drink, then asking me where I was from.

"England", I said.

"Yes, I can tell by your accent. Where in England?"

"London", I replied.

"Where in London?" she asked.

"Tufnell Park".

"Which end of Tufnell Park, the Holloway Road end or by Tufnell Park tube?"

I sat up, surprised. We chatted. About markets, about the street in Holloway where her sister had lived, about a London that she seemed to know as well as me. That I was a student, from SOAS, didn't seem to surprise her. Grace had worked at King's College and St Thomas' Hospital as a cleaner for short stints whilst she was in London. And when I explained why I was there, she suggested that two of the children who were hanging around us with intense curiosity should accompany me on a walk around the town before I continued my journey.

Bolanle, Ayomide and I set off from the market. We walked past the stalls stacked with brightly coloured plastic household items and cheap clothes, past market women crouched close to the ground selling pats of fufu, measures of dried cassava or containers of luminous orange palm oil, past Romeo's Cool Spot, a place I used to escape to, much later, for a cold beer at the end of dusty days, and along the crowded main street.

The sights of the town, for them - and later for me, when visitors came - were sites of tradition: the shrines of masquerades and the handful of Yoruba gods who had survived *atinga* and decades of neglect. We carried on walking, up through the winding paths of dense settlement to the large clearing where a market once sprawled and then down towards the forest to the grandiose, decaying palace that once housed the *Oba* (King) of Ilemi. As we went, people greeted us and laughed as I called back in Yoruba. One family, high up on the hill, beckoned me in and fed me a delicious soup, applauding my eagerness to eat it. Back in town, another family fended off my protestations and fed me again.

As we wound our way back to Grace's stall, I realised that I was falling for Ilemi. When the girls asked me if I was going to stay with them that night, I eagerly agreed. By the time I went with the children to sleep in a bunkbed in their room, my money bank wrap-around as a sheet, I had talked with Grace and her husband Bayo. We'd settled on a plan. I was to fetch my bags from Ibadan. There was a room in the old mud plaster family house with its rusted corrugated iron roof. I'd share the house with the children, a couple of young men who had been brought to town to go to school and help Bayo with farm work, Bayo's brother, Baba Tinu, and his wife, and another male relative and his wife – and, as I came to find out, a cage of noisy bush rats and an ambulant population of mice.

I'd wanted traditional. This would be it.

Anthropologists, I'd been led to believe, wandered around sampling potential field sites. They then made their decisions based on a list of criteria. It was, I'd been made to understand, a scientific decision, one taken with every rational consideration brought fully into view, the pros and cons carefully weighted.

Ilemi would have failed on every single criterion on my mental list entitled Essential Features of a Fieldsite. It was too large. Its population was too diverse a mixture of indigenes and those who townspeople called *alejo* (visitors), outsiders from elsewhere in Nigeria. Some were from the north or east of the country or from across the border in the Benin Republic. Some traced their ancestry back to settlers who arrived in the town in the chaos of the nineteenth century struggles between rival sub-ethnic kingdoms whose casualties had ended up as crowded cargo destined for the Americas. Most were Christian or Muslim. Ilemi's old shrines were largely derelict and the few that remained drew their devotees from among the elderly.

To crown it all, the town's ancestor god Alamuwa prohibited *Gelede*. In fact, I soon learned, the town had never once in all its history witnessed a *Gelede* performance.

But none of these rational criteria mattered any more. Ilemi had grabbed my heart and found a place in it. I knew instinctively that it was the right place. It was, I realised, the final nail in the coffin of my ill-conceived research project, bringing it to a decisive end. I hadn't quite figured out what would replace it. But I had found a Fieldsite.

I lay in my bunk in the darkness, the children fast asleep around me. I could hear the hubbub of the motorpark close by, with its steady stream of *danfos* and taxis, motors running as they disgorged visitors and inhabitants of the town alike at the entrance of the market. The idea of living in the very heart of the town appealed to me hugely. It surely wouldn't take me long to find a topic if I immersed myself in everyday life.

For the first time in weeks I felt that satisfying feeling that something that had been nagging away at me had been settled. I couldn't wait to get back to Ibadan, collect my bags, and get started. I might not have a project anymore. But I was an anthropologist. Anthropologists study everything. I had plenty of time. I would find something to write my thesis about. As I drifted off to sleep, I'd already moved into the little whitewashed room that was to be mine. I could picture myself at a desk at night writing fieldnotes by the light of a paraffin lamp.

Grace came to wake me in the morning. The children were already up, doing chores. I was overwhelmed by her and Bayo's generosity and kindness. When I was asked later why I'd chosen Ilemi, I told the truth: I'd rocked up one day looking for a drink, on my way to somewhere else, and the next thing I was moving in with the person who'd offered me a warm Coca Cola and then sent me to explore the town with her kids. And it really was that simple. There was something in the way we connected that clicked, and that was that.

I said my goodbyes, hugged the children and hopped into a waiting *danfo*, its door perilously wedged open. I clung for dear life onto the brown leatherette seatback as the vehicle navigated the pot holed road to Owode at break-neck speed. From there, I picked up a seat in a low-slung Peugeot 504 collective taxi bound for Ibadan.

As the car spirited us away from the border region, there weren't any roadblocks to negotiate. The road was a charcoal-coloured carpet of asphalt pitted with crags and craters that presented approaching vehicles with an obstacle course. The driver spun his wheel expertly, my stomach lurching as we rolled and wove through the potholes. We sped through dense, brilliant green tropical forest punctuated by small towns with the distinctive russet coloured mud-plaster traditional compounds, with their rusted iron roofs, and the new breezeblock houses that I came to know as 'storey buildings', with moats of hard-baked earth encasing their walled enclaves.

When I thought of those traditional anthropologists whose books I'd been made to read for my undergraduate degree in Social Anthropology, the image that formed in my mind was of spindly white men in khaki shorts and pith helmets. I pictured them roving around the tropical landscape on horseback or even being carried in litters as they searched for a fieldsite. The walls of the Royal Anthropological Institute in London were lined with their pictures. White men, every single one of them. The pictures brought back the flickering black and white films I'd watched on rainy Sunday afternoons as a child, with their stories of Africa as white man's dominion.

I knew there had been women anthropologists in those days. Some of them had made it onto my reading lists. Phyllis Kaberry. Audrey Richards. Margaret Mead. Ruth Benedict. And the one who had intrigued me the most, Zora Neale Hurston, poet, novelist, folklorist. I visualised them in frocks much like the flowery dresses I'd bought in Camden's second-hand shops in preparation for my fieldwork. I thought this was how a woman anthropologist ought to dress. I couldn't wear my usual black jeans and t-shirts. Those flowery dresses gave me, I felt, the air of someone who was a proper anthropologist. Someone to be entrusted with the stories that would soon fill my notebooks and become data.

In Ibadan, I gathered my possessions, the trappings of an anthropologist: a traveller's rucksack, crammed with books and flowery dresses. On a wafer-thin blue aerogram, I penned a message to my supervisor letting him know that I'd found a field site.

I wasn't quite ready to share the bad news about my project.

SETTLING IN

When I came back to Ilemi, I soon became aware of rumours circulating as to why I had come to the town and what I was doing. Some thought me to be a friend of Grace's from London. Others had me down as a wife or daughter of her husband Bayo from his days as an undergraduate student in Boston. As my friend Margaret later reminded me, to just turn up like that out of the blue was very odd. She herself thought I was a spy.

I'd expected to be mistaken for a missionary. I took especial pleasure in telling people that I followed the religion of the head of the household. Bayo was the town's only out atheist. But explaining what an anthropologist was remained a challenge. It's one that I've come to experience as universal. Once people get over the association between anthropologists and bones – "no, I'm not *that* kind of anthropologist, I prefer my humans alive," I'd tire of saying – the next most available stock image is of a white person emerging into the blazing African sun from a round, thatched roofed mud hut. They'd be carrying a small notebook in which they'd record the things they saw and heard, detailed accounts of rituals and customs and strange diagrams with lines, circles and triangles representing how people are related to each other - what anthropologists called 'kinship diagrams'.

As strangeness dissolved into familiarity and my antics no longer brought bemused stares and whispers, Ilemi became a home from home. From the first days, as I ventured into new parts of the town, marking places and faces in my mind, I was anchored by Grace and Bayo and their family. They gave me not just a space to live, but a place to be. The Yoruba name they later gave me captured the feeling I had of being in the right place: Ajoke, meaning someone everyone wants to pamper and look after. Angelica was too much of a mouthful. I became 'Ann' or 'Anna'. And the children knew me as 'Auntie Ann'.

The room Grace had offered me in the old mud plaster family house sat next to the foundations for a grand storey house that she and Bayo were in the process of building. To date, they'd got as far as finishing the basement. Wide concrete steps ran down into the earth, into a concrete lined room with a shiny floor. On one side was their bedroom with louvred windows letting in a sliver of light. On the other, a narrow set of stairs ran up to a bathroom with a flushable toilet, and a kitchen area with a floor crowded with large plastic storage containers, baskets used to collect vegetables and take pepper and tomato for grinding, and a large portable dual gas ring.

The main structure for the house was in place, with concrete steps running up to the first floor and a flight of steps around the side of the building leading to a flat concrete roof. In the months to come, I'd often sneak up there to a breeze-block perch to smoke a cigarette in peace, my presence concealed by the feathery green canopy of a large tree.

On market days, one day in every four, the town would swell with the influx of buyers and sellers from the surrounding rural villages and markets as far afield as those on the edges of Lagos. But there was also a quieter daily market, mostly selling everyday foodstuffs. Parallel to the market ran Ilemi's main street, scattered with small enterprises, iron mongers, a shop that sold paint where I went to buy emulsion to paint my room – a scene that drew spectators from the neighbourhood as the very idea of the white woman grown impatient with the efforts of the man who'd been brought in to whitewash the room, seizing a paintbrush and taking over the decoration herself, was just too odd and funny.

There were tailors and hairdressers in every quarter of the town. A giggling gaggle of identically dressed young women, apprentices to the craft, filled little stalls, sewing machines whirring and pedals pumping, mixing the chemicals to perm, straighten and dye hair, from dawn to dusk. On the walls were posters from the market with the season's designs or the fashion pictures featured on the back pages of women's magazines, with names like *Intimate Affairs* or *Hints*.

I was within a few minutes' reach of just about everything that there was to buy in the town. A barren stationery shop, scant stock scattered along its shelves, supplied me with notebooks. I'd taken to using book-keeping books for my fieldnotes. Large, almost square, with a dark blue cover and a thin sliver of blue carbon paper, they had numbered pages. They gave me a top copy with a serrated edge easy to tear off and bundle up to keep separately from the main copy. Like many anthropologists of my generation, I'd been brought up on tales of the one whose hut burnt down, razing their piles of fieldnotes. Srinivas' book *The Remembered Village*, written entirely from recall, was held up as a cautionary tale: this is what happens if you don't take precautions.

Along the main street from the market were several pharmacists, or more accurately, stalls selling dusty stacks of boxes of medicines of various provenances. At dusk, when the town livened into a frenetic pace, customers would crowd into these cramped, dimly lit, stalls seeking remedies. There was a one-shot handful of pills called *onisemejo* – literally, 'it works for eight', a cocktail of medicines that claimed to be a cure-all for eight sicknesses. Swallow the lot at night when you're aching, I was told, and you'll feel right as rain in the morning.

I bought a little sachet just to see. It was a heady mix. Librium and Valium to take the edge off things, chloroquine just in case it was malaria, paracetamol for aches and pains, iron and multivitamin to give your system a boost, an antacid and a tablet of chloramphenicol for good measure – an antibiotic that I knew only as a treatment for typhoid. It was some years later that I found out just how much of the medicine sold in these little shops was fake.

I made my little whitewashed room home. I had a clothes rail, on which I hung my magic blue *buba* and wrapper, the dollar bills safely still concealed in its hem. Grace had given me a shiny dresser with shelves, where I put my books. Over my bed was a voluminous mosquito net that I'd brought from London, prepared for the tropics. I tucked it in tight to keep out mosquitoes, mice, and any other unwanted visitors. It was like the dens I used to make out of sheets when I was little. Like I did as a child, I'd lie in bed at night reading by the light of my torch.

The mud plaster house baked in the daytime sun and the little window with its metal bars had to be closed at night to keep out night-time wildlife. A fan sat in the middle of my room like an ornament. It barely ever moved. More often than not there was no electricity. A big factory had been built down the line from the town, and the owner had reportedly paid handsome bribes to divert the power that should have come our way. Not for nothing had the Nigerian Electric Power Authority (NEPA) earned the name *Never Expect Power Always*. When the state enterprise was privatised under Structural Adjustment it became NEPA (plc). *Never Expect Power Always (please light a candle)*.

What breeze there was carried occasional gusts of fermenting cassava through the iron bars of my window. It was the most intensely nauseating smell I'd ever encountered. It was more pungent than the smell surfacing from the pit latrines behind the house or the pigs that Bayo kept in a nearby stall. It had an earthy putrid tone, overlain with a sharp scent of vomit that had an almost indecent sweetness to it. I could never quite get used to it. It reminded me of the dark beige stains seeping through the sawdust that was strewn over freshly lain piles of sick in the long wooden corridors at school. The smell would mingle with the thick odour of polish and travel under doors into the classroom.

Vats of fermenting cassava sat in compounds all over Ilemi. Their putrid-smelling contents would be dried, ground into a fine powder and made into a thick porridge called *fufu*. Just across from my room, women sat in rows on wooden benches packing handfuls of it into little pats covered in clingfilm, arranging them neatly on large woven trays to take to market. *Fufu* had a silkier texture than *eba*, which was made from fresh grated and roasted cassava ground into a coarse flour and mixed with water to make a lumpy liquid that turned almost translucent when it was heated. With deft movements of a wooden spoon, it would be scooped and turned and scraped and folded into a chewy, gooey mash.

Eba lacked the sharp tang and acrid odour of *fufu*, and became my daily staple, sticking on my fingers like wet bread dough when I broke off small balls to dip in rich stews of ground pepper, tomatoes, and onions, salty and fine.

My favourite of all was the third of Ilemi's staples: *iyan*, pounded yam made from huge tubers that looked like logs, deep brown fibrous and bark-like on the outside, translucent white within. *Iyan* was made in large carved mortars as high as the shins of the women who heaved huge wooden pestles to pummel the fibrous fruit into a smooth, thick paste with the texture of mashed potato. It tasted a bit like the 1970s British classic powdered mix, Smash. On a Sunday, Grace would boil yams for breakfast, serving them with a sweet sauce of scotch bonnet peppers, palm oil and tomato blended to a pulp and stirred over a hot flame until it was soft and sleek. It was utterly delicious.

Shades of colour like paint samples - grey-white, bright-white, old yellow white – distinguished the three in their cling-film wrapping, as they sat in neatly packed rows in the baskets that lined the roadside by the market. I knew them by how they felt as I dropped a small ball of the paste into my mouth: the acrid tang of *fufu,* the grainy stickiness of *gari,* the chewy smoothness of pounded yam.

Fufu, eba and *iyan* were a Nigerian version of ready meals. Working women could collect a bagful of cling-film wrapped pats to spare themselves that part of preparations for the evening's meal. A stew would have been made in the early morning, ground tomato and scotch bonnet pepper for the base, to which would be added smoked fish or dried meat, vegetables, sometimes some locust bean, and little yellow and red metal-wrapped cubes of Maggi. Returning home at dusk, they would drag a three-legged iron pot onto rekindled embers or a large fierce-flamed gas ring and bring the stew to a boil. They'd then send one of the children of the compound with a handful of Naira to collect enough pats for whoever was around for the evening's meal from one of the many places in the neighbourhood where women vendors plied their trade. Rapidly de-shelled from their plastic casing with an expert flick of the wrist, the pat of *fufu, eba* or *iyan* would be peeled onto a plate and served with a dollop or two of stew.

These are the kind of details I recorded faithfully in my fieldnotes. I'd had little guidance as to what these notes should contain, other than that I should write a daily diary and record everything I'd seen and heard that day. I instilled in myself a practice of sitting by the light of a paraffin lamp transcribing the hastily written fragments from the day's discoveries in the little reporter's book I carried with me into those large blue record books, a leaf of blue carbon creating a detachable second copy of each page. These I'd faithfully bundle up and send to my supervisor in London to keep safe for me.

Into these notebooks I poured all my curiosities, the flicker of an idea of how it might all fit together and the frustration of finding out that it didn't. I thought that by writing everything down, I'd be sure not to miss something that could turn out to be important later. Vital clues. Promising leads. I had no clue at this stage what could replace my lost project. I tried not to think too hard about that. Instead, I focused on organising myself like a proper researcher should. I gave each of the record books a letter of the alphabet, so that its hundred numbered pages could be coded. I had a little red box of notecards with topics and the numbers and codes for each. I'd look back over them to seek out connections and double-back on lines of enquiry that I hadn't yet exhausted. The codes told their own stories. Markets, local: A22, D55-56. Witches: A34, B33, C66-72. Love medicine: B44-60, D21-25.

STANLEY, I PRESUME?

As I settled into my fieldwork, there were a few other practical matters to which I needed to attend. I'd become adept at wedging my body into any available space in those battered brown and yellow Toyota passenger vans called *danfo*. People would shriek to see the foreigner. They'd shout *"oyinbo ni!"* when the sliding door rolled open and they clap eyes on me sitting there, jammed between my fellow passengers, smiling. On my trips to Lagos to cash in one of the stache of $100 bills stitched into my wrapper, I'd been struck at how often the conductors waived my money away. It was so rare to find an *oyinbo* riding a *danfo*. Once, boarding a *danfo* in mainland Lagos, I even had my fare paid by a soldier in fatigues and wraparound sunglasses, his face melting into a broad grin when I cheerfully greeted my fellow passengers in Yoruba.

As the weeks went by, I found myself harbouring an increasingly intense desire for a vehicle of my own. A car was, I put it to myself, necessary. I would, I reasoned, be so much safer. I would personally supervise its maintenance. I'd be able to rest assured that it had functioning brakes, tyres with adequate thread and bodywork constructed out of metal rather than filler. I'd already seen too many accidents where what had seemed like metal seconds before crumpled like a thin leaf of paper scrunched up to throw into the bin. I applied for a loan from the University of London. By return, I received notice that it had been granted.

I started looking around. I had a very particular model in mind:

a Peugeot 504, old enough to have the cachet of being vintage-looking, sturdy enough not to need too extensive renovation, bashed up enough to be unappealing to thieves and car jackers. For all the advice to get myself one of those cheap Japanese imports that had begun to filter into the market, I was holding firm.

There seemed to be plenty of suitable 504s plying the roads. But finding the right one rapidly become a hapless quest. I'd trail around the second-hand car yards of Ibadan on every visit there. But I had no idea what to look for in a car. Especially the kind of cars that were for sale here, vehicles that had been sent for scrap in Europe and then bundled into trailers bound for Lagos. There they would languish rusting in the docks, awaiting the right backhander to be slipped to the right person to secure their release in a flurry of spurious paperwork. Freed to go, they would be driven up the Lagos-Ibadan expressway, past the prayer camps and the carcasses of the accidents that made that road a legendary danger, to weave through the outskirts and into the unruly muddle of rusty vehicles that littered the city's used car yards.

After several weeks of looking, I had been forced to adjust my expectations sharply downwards. For one thing, these cars were expensive. I'd taken a blue 504 out for a spin, felt the softness of the brakes, the indistinct slide of the gearbox, the crunchiness beneath my feet where the chassis had started to give way, and looked with utter amazement at the dealer when he said he'd do a 'special price' of £1,000. There were cheap Mazdas and Nissans and even the occasional VW, but Peugeot 504s were pricey. By then, though, there was no dissuading me.

It was not love at first sight, but when the bronze metallic 504 with its burgundy velour seats was driven into the yard of the Lebanese fixer who promised me that he'd find me what I was looking for, I did at least pause to admire something of its stature. The colour wasn't right. Too brash. It was more recent a model than the ones I'd coveted. Too ugly. But by that stage I'd come to realise that I'd better cut my losses. I lugged a rucksack full of Naira halfway across town to make the purchase, solemnly counting out the blue and green notes in tidy piles on the table in the merchant's office.

The car was mine.

Before I could drive it away, I had to give it a name. The first one that came into my head made me smile. Then laugh out loud. My chuckles attracted the stares of the men sitting in the back of the office in their white robes.

Stanley. The car would be Stanley.[2]

Acquiring Stanley had been easy enough. But to drive him away, I would need to get a driving license. Before I left London, I'd been advised to learn to drive. Having never believed it possible, I'd passed my test. My success amazed my teacher, a squat red-haired man with an unappealing habit of picking flecks of dried skin out of his beard as I sat beside him behind the wheel. He had no confidence in my abilities.

"He's the worst of the lot," he muttered as we sat in the waiting room for the driving test, eyeing my test examiner as he strode impatiently into the room to get the paperwork.

Afterwards, as I basked in the glory of having passed first time, I made a point of not sharing with my driving teacher all those tall tales told to my examiner about the dangers of travelling alone to *deepest darkest* West Africa, and the protections from the hazards of the road that having my own car might offer.

After all that, I wouldn't be able to drive in Nigeria until I'd gone through the whole rigmarole again. But this was, after all, Nigeria. In Nigeria, many things are possible.

"I just took my test in London," I said to my fixer, "Does this mean I need to take it again? Will I need lessons to learn how to drive the way people drive here?"

He roared with laughter. I later realised quite how funny the idea of an *oyinbo* asking for lessons to learn how to drive like a Nigerian must have seemed, but at the time I just didn't get what he was finding so hilarious.

"No, no, don't you worry. Just bring a photo," he said.

"What for?" I asked.

"For your driving license. They will need a photo."

I went off to a photo shop and secured the photo. I took it to the fixer. I was told to return the next day. Sure enough, when I arrived the next day my driving license was ready. A black-and-white photo of a tired-looking light brown-haired white woman in a flowery dress was stapled onto a test certificate. The certificate was peppered with ticks and scribbles, a detailed account of the performance of the candidate in the photograph in the road test. She had, I saw, done very well, although there were a few places where there was clearly scope for improvement.

I had license to drive.

I got into Stanley for the first time, settled myself into the carpeted expanse of the driving seat, pulled the door shut, reached for my seat belt, and put the keys in the ignition.

THE ACCIDENT

"Insurance?"

The burly man, resplendent in a light pink lace *agbada*, looked at me and roared with laughter. I'd looked up the offices of the insurance company whose jingles I'd seen on the TV. It took me some while to find, and I'd parked Stanley gingerly in the parking lot outside.

It had been quite a nerve-wracking experience to be thrust into the middle of Ibadan's traffic uninsured.

"You askin' for insurance? This is Nigeria-o!"

I pointed to the badly printed leaflet in my hand, promising me two kinds of insurance scheme with all the benefits one would expect.

"But it says here that comprehensive insurance is available,"

"Available, yes. Available means you pay. Not they pay you."

I took all of five minutes to weigh up the risks of an accident against the chances of the insurance company paying up.

Third party insurance it was.

Stanley sat gleaming bronze in the late afternoon sun of the car park behind the insurance company's offices. I turned the key. The engine leapt alive and settled into a gentle purr.

They say that you can see a car crash in slow motion, like you're in a film and time grinds to a virtual halt and then moves towards you, frame by frame. But this one had nothing of that smoothness to it. Snatched out of conversation by a brutal bolt of screeching brakes, the smell of rubber on the wet asphalt, the screams of those who soon dashed to surround the scene, I was flung forward and wrenched back as my seatbelt tensed to save me.

An oily, burnt smell hung thickly in the air. I sat there in stunned silence. The scene gradually came into view. A man lay on the ground in front of the car's crumpled bumper, his bike wheels whirring. He rolled onto his side, groaning, then sprang to his feet and dusted himself off. I breathed hard with relief. I'd heard the apocryphal tales of white people crashing cars into people and finding themselves on the wrong side of an angry mob.

Suddenly, as if out of nowhere, the car was surrounded with people. I felt the chill of fear begin to creep through my body. But the crowd was not angry. Just curious. Children jostled with each other for a glimpse of the *oyinbo* sitting behind the wheel of a car that was so old and badly resprayed, it added to the oddity of the scene. White people didn't travel in cars like this. White people generally didn't drive their cars themselves. You'd see them sitting in the back of a big, brand-new Toyota four-wheel drive, whisked seamlessly between air-conditioned offices, hotels, and homes without ever imbibing the raucous vitality of the country they were in. And there I was, sitting in stunned silence, staring into the middle distance as the crowd began to thicken.

I'd never been in an accident before. It wasn't anything like I'd been told to expect.

I needed a cigarette. I opened the door and stepped into the crowd, hurrying towards a woman seated behind a basket of snacks, cigarettes, and candles. With a brazen smile in her eyes, she charged me five times the usual price for a cigarette.

"How now?" I asked.

"You need it, ma'am," was her response.

As I walked back to the car, I caught sight of a man in a flowing white agbada step through the crowds and make his way towards the wrecked vehicle. I could have hugged him. My guardian angel. Bayo was here and he'd sort everything out. He soon began barking orders to have the car towed.

"But" I protested, "don't we need to call the police?"

He roared with laughter. "The police?"

"Don't we need to notify them? Of the accident?"

I carried on insisting that we call the police, rebuffing the laughter, shrugs, and protestations that it would only complicate matters.

The police would, he said, impound the car and charge us to release it.

But I wouldn't let it go. I knew I was being very British, but it was hard-wired into me that in a situation like this, you needed to call the police otherwise they'd be calling on you, and then you'd really be in trouble.

"We'll call them, then," he eventually conceded. "And then you'll see."

Half an hour later, two policemen arrived at the scene. One took out a tape measure and proceeded to measure the width of the road.

"International standard," he announced.

They then tied the car up and impounded it.

It took a week to get the car back. I had to pay a release fee, as predicted. Bayo sent an ox to drag it home along the pockmarked road, through the iridescent green fields of sugar cane, yam, and oil palm. I was sitting with the children on long, dusty bench outside the family house at dusk when the ox came into view, a thick rope looped round its body, pulling Stanley behind him.

The road might have been international standard, but my first crash was most definitely Nigerian.

INVENTING MRS MAINSTREAM

A car of many lives, many resprays, Stanley's innards were a bricolage that bore the traces of the ingenuity of West African mechanics who could fashion impermanent solutions out of just about anything at hand. Bronze metallic veneer neatly covered the patches of filler that had come to be substituted for more expensive metal. Stanley was often off the road with ailments that consumed large bundles of Naira and hours in the hot sun of the mechanic's yard. He had a temperamental carburettor, a radiator that had never recovered from the crash, and a dodgy gearbox. But having Stanley was a notch up from not having a car at all. And I soon found myself being remonstrated with for not using him more often.

"Ann," Margaret would chastise me, "you should not be going here and there in the sun like that. Think of what people will say about you. A woman like you should be taking a motor, not walking along the roadside like an ordinary person."

Margaret owned a hotel on the outskirts of the town. It was far enough for me to need Stanley's help to get there if I wasn't feeling brave enough for one of the little passenger motorbikes called *okada*. It was somewhere where I could retreat to drink a cold beer, smoke a cigarette and unwind. Margaret had spent years living in London and had family there. She and Grace had become my wise women. I'd bring dilemmas to them, seek their advice, and heed their admonishments.

It wasn't just the car that was the problem. My dress sense was appalling. I'd abandoned the flowery dresses and gone instead, with the penchant of a foreigner, for *bubas* and wrappers made from the hand-dyed cloth sold in the market in Abeokuta. Rough stuff worn by those with neither style nor money, in my friends' eyes.

"Ann, look at that dress. How can you go out with that cloth? People will talk. A woman like you should be dressing properly. Let us go and buy some guinea brocade or lace to make you something better."

But I resisted. I didn't want to be a Big Woman. My whiteness gave me a big-ness that I battled without success to displace. Swanning around the place in my car wearing an expensive outfit was not my style. It also wasn't what an anthropologist was supposed to do. I thought back to those pith-helmeted white men in shorts in the Royal Anthropological Institute's hallway. Would they have donned suits to do fieldwork?

For quite some while, I entertained the belief that what I wore would help me *fit in*; a simple *buba* and wrapper in local fabric seemed like the way to go. I'd always hated flowery dresses in any case. My belief extended to the rather wishful thought that if I wore clothes that were like those worn by most other women, I might not draw too much attention to myself. *As if* being the only white woman in town wasn't going to be enough to attract anyone's attention, whatever I wore.

Eventually, I gave in and bought up an armful of lengths of block-printed cloth in the market in Abeokuta. To please Grace and Margaret, I added a few six-yard pieces of guinea brocade in my favourite colours, turquoise, cerise and mulberry.

Grace called a tailor to the house. When I described what I wanted – a simple *buba*, wrapper and head tie – Grace and the tailor went into animated conference in Yoruba, amidst a cloud of tut-tutting. Instructions were then issued by Grace. The tailor spun me around her tape measure and disappeared into her crowded shop near the market. Two days later, she emerged with a pile of neatly folded and pressed fashion creations.

My mother would have been proud of me, I thought to myself, as I put on matching top and pleated skirt. It was the perfect marriage of flowery dress and local cloth. The design was clearly not shop-bought. It was some strange European-local hybrid. It all added up to an image of a foreigner who had lived in this country for some while. There remained the possibility that I was the wife of a Nigerian man who had travelled abroad and brought me back with him. That would explain the car.

It was the perfect disguise for the character I was perfecting: Mrs Mainstream.

I needed Mrs Mainstream for a variety of purposes. I had it in my head that such a persona was necessary for me to cultivate if I were to be a proper anthropologist, even without the flowery dresses. I'd begun thinking about impression management in encounters with the various armed officials I'd meet on the road on trips out of town. Gone was the ruse of covering my whiteness with my head-tie. Travels with Stanley would give me no option but to reveal my face.

Either it was my sartorial choices or Stanley himself, but the police and border officials would rarely hassle me as much as in the days when I seemed to be simply a tourist passing through. The fact that I was driving myself, rather than being driven - as were other white people who very occasionally sped through the inland route to the border with Benin - won me plaudits, along with the raised eyebrows and amused faces I'd see as I drove through small villages and hamlets.

Over time I became accustomed to joking with the police. My friends found it disconcerting. They'd tell me in hushed voices that in this Nigeria, it wasn't good to treat the police in this way. But I persisted. I'd found it got me through the checkpoints as fast as when I could cover my head and pretend. There was something about cracking jokes with those whose arbitrary exercise of power might otherwise turn malign, as if to defuse them, disarm them. It lightened the situation. Instantly.

I became positively cheeky.

One day, I'd decided to take a short cut through the back roads to Abeokuta and ran into a small band of police officers. They'd set up a make-shift police post by the side of the narrow dirt road and were stopping cars with the purpose, I imagined, of collecting some rent in the form of bribes. As soon as they saw the white face driving towards them, they rushed out into the road waving their arms to flag me down. Four of them surrounded the car. It was a hot day. Stanley had no air-conditioning, and I'd taken to winding down all the windows to keep a breeze circulating.

Eight hands reached simultaneously into the car.

"Show your papers!" one of the policemen shouted.

I knew exactly what they were up to. To their upturned hand, I added mine. And, with a big smile on my face, I said the unthinkable.

"*Fun-mi l'owo!*" Give me money!

It was a very risky quip. For a split second, I thought I had badly misjudged the moment. But no. They roared with laughter, patting their hands on the roof of the car with mirth. Then they stepped away from the car.

"Ah Madam, you can go now!"

These encounters with officialdom affirmed the value of travelling under the assumed persona of Mrs Mainstream. The more conventional my outfit, the easier my interactions seemed to become.

So far, so good. But my metamorphosis was not yet complete. Next, I needed a respectable profession.

If I was a teacher, I could answer people's questions about what I was doing there with, "I'm a teacher." So simple. Everyone would immediately get it. As a teacher from another country, I could then say that I was familiarising myself with Nigerian culture and that's why I was to be found in the town asking people questions about everything and anything.

I applied at the local secondary school for a job as a volunteer teacher. *Voluntourists*, those who visit themselves on African school children with no training whatsoever, represent a particular kind of colonial hangover; the idea that white people innately know how to teach *because they must know better* and they would be able to simply set foot in the classroom, untutored and unprepared, *because they must know better.*

Don't get me wrong. I'd been one of those white people myself. Escape from Thatcher's Britain had taken me to the wide-open skies of post-revolution Zimbabwe. It had turned into a longer stay than I'd had in mind when I set off in search of adventure. By the time I arrived in Nigeria, I had almost two years of secondary school teaching under my belt. Lesson plans, marking, small group teaching in large mixed ability classes, I considered myself to be almost a professional.

THE LESSON

First thing on Monday morning I reported for duty. St Botulph's was on the other side of town. I decided this was an occasion on which I ought to display my respectability by taking Stanley. I gave Iya Dayo the day off, smoothed out my most proper flowery dress, and washed and styled my hair. I wanted to look as much Mrs Mainstream as possible.

Stanley rolled gently through the pockmarked road from the market to the junction, where the sound of touts calling for custom for *danfos* plying the route sang out throughout the day. Purring, Stanley made his way down the hill to the lush, verdant riverside, over the bridge and then up the steep slope towards the Catholic church. The church sat at the highest-most place in the town. It was an austere looking building made of grey stone, crowned with a frowning statue of Jesus. I had no idea who St Botulph had been but imagined him to be as grim and joyless as the building.

The school was right next to the church and was built of red mud bricks and mortar, with wide pathways neatly edged with white-painted stones. The school yard was fringed with mature trees, their feathery leaves providing a green umbrella of shade for children to linger under during breaks. A semblance of a lawn sat in the middle of the quad formed by the classroom buildings, straggly patches of green on red clay soil. Children filed towards the entrance, a large arch with a sign bearing the name of the school in thin black lettering and a crest with a motto. They were dressed in identical green and white checked gingham, with matching dark green canvas bags on their backs. They pointed and giggled when they saw me drive by and then gasped with astonishment as I drew my car up outside the school, parking it under a tree.

"Where's the headmaster's office?" I asked one of the children.

They looked terrified at coming up so close to a white woman. I'd become aware of hard my accent was to understand. I consciously avoided doing the English-person-addressing-a-foreigner routine of saying exactly the same thing, but louder and slower. Instead, I took to using a range of accents until I hit on one that helped the other person understand. For this small child, it was broad Mancunian.

I was brought up in the north east of England, a land of many and varied accents; a true north easterner can place a dialect within a matter of miles. When my parents moved south when I was a teenager, I was surrounded by people who found my accent what they described as "quaint". "Is that what they say in the North?" I'd be asked, with that most southern English of insinuations that it *wasn't quite* how one ought to pronounce what I'd just said. This struck terror into me. For a while, I clammed up completely; as long as I didn't open my mouth, I reasoned, I wouldn't be treated to that gentle, mocking, rebuke when I said things wrong.

Later, when I worked in a call centre in London phoning people at random from torn-out pages from telephone directories to ask them questions about their preferences in consumer goods, I entertained myself by practising different accents. By then, I could slip easily from broad north-east into posh south-east. I was especially fond of a Manchester accent and worked hard on getting it right. I had a weakness for Scottish accents of all kinds, from Glaswegian rough diamonds to the soft burr of the lavender-haired lady from the Highlands who lived up our road when I was a child. Once I phoned up an old man in Dundee who couldn't understand a word of what I was saying until I shifted gear into a take-off of the lavender lady.

For all that I'd played with pronunciation, I never imagined that one day I would be standing in front of a class of Nigerian children teaching them how to speak like the Queen.

I hadn't quite registered that by putting myself forward as a volunteer, I could be quite legitimately asked to help with whatever needed doing. The headmaster had plans for me. Despite it being almost thirty years after the end of colonial rule, there was still part of the Nigerian English language curriculum that required students to study English pronunciation. And Nigerian English it was not. Instead, prescribed in the textbook that was handed to me, was what those who speak it call *received pronunciation*.

Lesson one. The headmaster introduced me to the class, who stared at me agog. I imagine that they, too, had never seen an *oyinbo* at such close range. And then he left me to get on with it.

I opened the text book and eyed the phonetics. I imagined myself saying, "Now children, repeat after me. The kæt sæt on the mæt."

And then I tried to do just that.

I opened my mouth. The words would not come. I tried again. I just couldn't. I *really* couldn't. And then something I hadn't expected to happen popped out. A large, involuntary guffaw. I dissolved in a pile of giggles. The children looked at me, wide-eyed. This *oyinbo* that no-one could understand, standing there laughing and laughing and laughing.

It was a kind of proper that I couldn't muster, even when dressed like Mrs Mainstream and trying my very best to oblige.

The children were silent for a while, then burst into a noisy chatter.

"What's going on?" boomed the headmaster, putting his head around the door and frowning.

"I just... I just can't," I said. "I can't do this."

He shot me a quizzical look.

"Come to my office, Miss Sorel," he said, "and we will deal with this there."

I explained why I'd failed so spectacularly at the project he'd had for me. The headmaster nodded as I made my long apology. He understood. I was reprieved. I was still to teach English language, but without the pronunciation.

And so began the first of many days of enjoyment. I had a purpose. I could explain what I was doing in the town, "I'm here to teach," I'd say, and it was instantly explicable. Teaching fell directly within the narrow range of what it was that white people did in Nigeria. Not missionary. *Teacher*. It was an identity to identify with. It saved me those awkward conversations in which I tried to explain how it was that my government had paid for me to spend my days wandering around town asking people all manner of nosy questions. Now I was a teacher, my question-asking became like a hobby, something I did after work. People began asking me if school had finished yet if I arrived on their porches before mid-afternoon, insinuating that I must be slacking and knocking off work early.

Meanwhile, at school, teaching was becoming anthropological fieldwork. My classes failed to follow any prescribed form. I'd come to believe that the key to learning how to write English well was to write as frequently as possible and have someone with a sympathetic eye go over the writing and mark up mistakes with a red pen. Not the chastising red pen that corrects every error. But one that's a helper, that points out where a conjugation doesn't quite work, where the correspondence between the elements of the sentence isn't quite right, and that offers lots of encouragement and praise.

I revelled in my work. There's little more satisfying than having a class full of enthusiastic, bright young minds turn their imaginations to making up stories. Sometimes, I'd get them to turn their tales into skits to perform to the class, then instruct them to write them up for their homework. On occasion, I'd set them topics. At other times, I let them choose what they wanted to write about.

From my teaching, I got a glorious collection of episodes from everyday life to add to my ethnographic explorations. I set the students to write about witches, and they wrote essays distinguishing between witches of different hues – white, red, and black – who had a propensity for good as well as for evil. Their stories about love and romance gave me vital insights into the role of resources in relationships. I asked them to interview their grandmothers about their lives, and their compositions told with affection and admiration of women who'd worked tirelessly and found, in their old age, the joys of being surrounded by their people. I marked enthusiastically, looking forward to the next instalment. Their grammar and spelling improved in leaps and bounds.

For all that I was enjoying myself, after a matter of weeks I had to come to the sad realisation that I was spending my evenings with piles of exercise books rather than writing up my fieldnotes. I wasn't going to make the most assiduous teacher if I was to get on with my research. My days at St Botulph's became a short-lived pleasure. But they introduced me to the town in a way nothing else could have done.

LOST IN TRANSLATION

Like a good British social anthropologist, I'd started my Yoruba classes at SOAS. I'd applied for additional time and funding for my PhD on the grounds that Yoruba fell within the category of 'difficult languages'. I'd taken with me to Nigeria a textbook written by a British scholar whose work I revered, Karin Barber, who spoke Yoruba so fluently she'd written the textbook *Yorùbá Dùn Ún So* to teach people like me. I tried my very best to cultivate a daily habit of learning vocabulary. I forced myself to sit down and work through by rote conjugations, tenses, stock phrases I might need to use in everyday social situations. But when people burst into voluble chatter around me, I could never follow what was going on.

I'd learnt Portuguese by a process of osmosis on languid Bahian nights spent bathing in the warmth of the language and days spent sitting in the shade soaking up the sounds around me. I'd sing along to João Gilberto and Vinicius de Moraes and other Bossa Nova favourites, gradually disentangling phrases, recognising words by repetition and noting their placement in a sentence. I'd comb the newspaper, spotting the patterns made by words with roots I could recognise. Within months, I was virtually fluent.

This experience had given me a false confidence in my language learning capacities. Unfortunately, I found myself completely out of my depth with Yoruba. Juju and Fuji music were so fast and furious, I couldn't make out a single word. Fela sang mainly in English. Highlife made my hips sway, but I didn't glean a single word from many hours of listening to it. Newspapers were in English. The only written Yoruba near at hand was the Bible, and even if I'd wanted to read it, I knew I wouldn't be able to make head or tail of it.

Yoruba is a language whose tonal inflections, I was to find, gave a new edge to *double entendre*. The word *oko* had the most expansive of semantic ranges when dots were added to either or both 'o'. *Oko* means farm, *ọkọ* means husband, and *okó* means penis. The prospect of mispronunciation made both husbands and farms a delicate topic. I hadn't expected either of them to feature much in my fieldwork, but I was soon to find all three making an appearance in the conversations I ended up having.

A few weeks in, my home-administered Yoruba lessons were not going well. I was bored of learning from the book. No-one understood me when I stuttered the clutch of new words that I'd learnt that day. Or else they'd look at me with pity. There was something about my whiteness that evoked that kind of tolerant sympathy, rather than inviting the ridicule that my efforts might have warranted. Impatience got the better of me. Technically, I reasoned, I was going to learn better by listening and then hearing the language in translation.

It was time to get an interpreter.

Interpreters are anthropologists' trade secret. Euphemistically referred to as 'field assistants', their presence is often entirely unremarked in the works anthropologists write, which are called *ethnographies*. Ethno-graphy: writing about a people. Anthropologists gain their authority as producers of knowledge through a form of writing that is liberally scattered with reminders to the reader of the anthropologist having *been there*. Not for nothing is the main method of the anthropologist, hanging out with people, dignified with the technical term 'participant observation'.

The founding father of social anthropology's fieldwork method, Bronislaw Malinowski, had gone off in a boat with a tent and some notebooks and come back a couple of years later brimming full of insights about how the men in a distant Papua New Guinean atoll conducted their economic and sexual lives. His magnum opus was a tale of an elaborate skein of exchange relations, which he had come across by participating and observing, painstakingly piecing it all together. It took a couple of decades and a woman anthropologist, Annette Weiner, to surface a side of the Trobriand Island exchange rituals that Malinowski missed or disregarded, so focused was he on the ways of men. It involved transacting huge bundles of banana leaves and fibre skirts: women's wealth.

Another one of anthropology's founding fathers, E.E. Evans-Pritchard studied the administration to chickens of a potent substance, *benge*, by the Sudanese Azande to determine the answers to questions about the culpability of people accused of committing such acts as adultery or witchcraft. If the chicken lived, the alleged perpetrator was innocent. If it died, then it was proof. Only a special ritual facilitator, the *puta benge*, could supervise the ritual and only under strict conditions that included celibacy and avoiding fart-inducing vegetables and strong-smelling meats. On the other side of the world, in Bali, the American cultural anthropologist Clifford Geertz described in the finest of detail the traditional Balinese cockfight and with it the complex relationships men had with their cocks and their masculinities, coining the term 'thick description' in the process.

All this and more can be possible, I'd come to understand, when you learn the language. The lesson I took from all of this is what you come to know about a place depends on who you talk with, and who will talk with you. Speaking the language was surely a way in which people would tell you stuff that wasn't just playing a game with the ignorant foreigner asking stupid questions. I secretly wondered how many anthropologists actually managed to pull this off. Did they really all speak other languages so fluently that they understood people's innermost thoughts and could grapple with apparently entirely different concepts of time, matter, and existence? I had sneaking doubts.

Scientists have their experiments, literature specialists have their close readings of literary works, historians their archives. But anthropology relies for its authenticity as well as for its data on hanging out, tuning in, and figuring out what is going on. Imagine if you couldn't understand a word of what people were saying and had to go away and try and figure it out afterwards. I wondered how often that happened as anthropologists sat scribbling fieldnotes in longhand by the light of their paraffin lamps.

I loved the sound of Yoruba. I was mesmerised when the talking drummers would take to the streets or arrive to a ceremony dressed in delicately woven *aso oke agbadas* made of cloth threaded through with gold, wedging their drums to their sides with their elbows and beating them expertly with sticks shaped like an elongated thumb, mimicking the tones of the language. You could literally hear them chattering, complaining, praising or demanding.

When my children were babies, I'd surprise them out of their tears by breaking into a long stream of Yoruba, using words I'd first heard drummed, the popping noise of ọ and ẹ and the low, deep, guttural sound of *gb*. I'd incant the phrases used around me time and again in Ilemi. *Obinrin ko se gbekele. Eja gbigbe ni. O se o. M'ogbo die die. Bayo ni. Se alaafia ni.* "More! More!" they'd cry as they got older and I'd chant them out of their tantrums or doldrums, raising a laugh as I broke into those familiar Yoruba phrases. And I'd tell them about what it was like to be having a conversation with a talking drum, and about the Egungun masquerades that I'd come to associate with those drums, all swirling primary colours and the fizzing excitement of the children, high with the thrill of the dancing figures darting in and out of the crowd, the sheer magic of it all.

The truth of the matter is that for all the lessons and the efforts, I never got beyond the basics with Yoruba. It takes a brave or foolish anthropologist to admit it, but there it was. Instead, I found Iya Dayo, a doughty woman in her 50s with a penchant for religious lyrics and a propensity for lecturing young women about their morals. She was not my first choice. I'd latched on to a young Lagosian who'd wound up in Ilemi due to a bad boyfriend choice, her fluent English accompanied by a taste for bright lipstick, high heels, and flirtation. I liked her feistiness. I thought she'd be thoroughly unreliable, and we'd have a lot of fun.

"Ann, we need to talk." Grace had a very serious look on her face.

We went to my room.

When we got there, Grace started.

"That woman! You can't go around with her. What are people going to think of you? She is one of those 'eat and run' girls. Everyone can see. It will be shame for you."

"But all I need is someone to translate for me." I folded my arms. I wasn't giving up this easily.

"You think it's just about translation. But people will be watching you if they see you with a woman like that, they will not want to tell you any of their secrets."

She had a point.

"What am I going to do now?" I said.

"Find someone respectable." Grace knew she was right, as usual.

I still had no real idea of what I was going to be researching, so I needed to hedge my bets. What I needed, I realised, was a Nigerian equivalent of Mrs Mainstream. But where was I going to find her? I began to visualise the type of woman Grace had in mind. She'd need to be female. Preferably middle-aged. Almost certainly Christian. She'd have been married, possibly widowed. A retired schoolteacher would be perfect.

I found my ideal interpreter through the tendency I have always had to chat with strangers. It's something I've always thought meant I was destined to be an anthropologist, even before I knew what one was. I can literally chat to anyone, anywhere, about anything. I don't so much as chat as venture a couple of questions, smiling all the while, and people begin talking to me. It's a habit formed in the days when there was nothing else to distract me for long hours on public transport. It's sometimes a bit of a liability. But it has its uses.

One day, soon after having regretfully bade the feisty Lagosian goodbye, I was picking up a prescription at the hospital in Abeokuta. As I leaned on the counter of the pharmacy window, I chatted with the woman counting out pills into a little paper envelope. Curious about this white woman asking questions, she asked a few of her own. She established that I was a student, looking for someone who lived in or near Ilemi who could work for me as an interpreter. I established that she had a cousin, a retired teacher, who might well be interested in a part-time job.

I turned up at Iya Dayo's door, in a neat row of squat houses on an agricultural settlement close to Ilemi, later that afternoon. Within minutes the arrangements were made.

I had an interpreter. Now I could get started in earnest.

But there was a hitch. I still didn't have much of a clue about what my research would be about. This created a new dilemma. Iya Dayo wanted to know more about the job.

"You'll need to translate for me when I ask people questions," I said, "and we'll chat after we've talked with them about how it went, how you felt they responded, whether the questions were the put in the right way to make them feel they could answer freely, that kind of thing".

If it sounded a bit vague as a job description, that's because I was a bit vague myself.

"But what would we be asking about?" she asked.

"Life in Ilemi," I said.

"What about life in Ilemi?" she said, "what is it that you want to know?"

"Oh, you know…" I began and then realised that not only did she not know, but I didn't either. I had not yet recovered from the loss of my topic.

"We'll ask people questions about their lives," I said. "I'm an anthropologist," I said. "An anthropologist finds out about people's lives." That wasn't very convincing. She shot me a quizzical look, as if she would in theory be happy to indulge me, but it might not be a bad idea to know what she was letting herself in for.

Then I hit on an idea. Maybe the way to do this was to enlist Iya Dayo in helping me find a topic.

"What would you ask people questions about, if you were the one who was studying?". She gave me a stare as if to say *really, you've come all this way to Nigeria to do your research and you're asking me??*

And then she answered: "what women do to make money."

"OK, then," I said, "let's start there."

MONEY, MONEY, MONEY

Our first forays did not go according to plan. Iya Dayo made it plain from the start that simply conveying words from Yoruba to English like for like without comment was not going to be her style. This was a problem because, at least to begin with, my approach to interviewing was heavily influenced by having been formally trained.

I'd learnt about the construction of interview schedules, checklists, and semi-structured interview checklists. I had designed surveys, spending ages thinking about the kinds of numbers I'd want to collect and how to ask the question in such a way as to not pre-empt the response. I'd wondered in the process how researchers who just asked the kinds of questions that would give them numbers – yes or no, agree or disagree, how many - learnt unexpected things, or got to figure out whether their questions were worth asking in the first place.

One pressing question was who we'd interview and how we'd find them. My anthropological training hadn't had much to say about this, but I was familiar with sampling from my days working in market research. Random sampling involved practices like pulling names from a hat or interviewing every fifth woman in the neat rows of vendors selling tomatoes or cloth in the market or stopping at the porch of every fifth compound in a straight line from our house to the river. I'd always wondered about what researchers might have learnt if they'd chosen every third or every sixth. Was experience ever this uniform?

Purposive sampling felt too close to hand-picking people. I liked the idea of snowball sampling, building up a sample by people suggesting other people who'd be good to interview. There was something about it that invited people into the enquiry, offering them an opportunity to shape it by directing the researcher to their next conversation.

So far so good. The next challenge was how we'd do the interviews. I instinctually disliked hemming in conversations by having a pre-established list of topics or questions. I'd found it made the people less open and interviews far less interesting. I much preferred to strike out with a broad-brush account of what I was interested in hearing about, then throw the whole thing wide open and follow the lead of the person or people being interviewed.

Sometimes I would do a quick summary of the kinds of things I'd been finding out about up to that point, to kick things off. This was valuable for getting part the idiotic foreigner syndrome: it showed I had a bit of an idea of what was going down. People would react to what I said, to affirm or challenge it, and this got us into conversations that went deeper within minutes than I could get to if I started with polite generalities, far faster than working up through a pat patter of identical questions. For all I knew, this violated every single protocol known to the qualitative social scientist.

But it worked.

Despite all the thought I'd put into interviewing, I hadn't anticipated what to do if faced with a voluble or disapproving interpreter. Especially one who clearly had the kind of views that might silence those with whom I wanted to communicate. Disagreeing or indeed disagreeable field assistants were nowhere to be seen in the texts I'd pored over before going to 'the field'.

Ultimately, after attempts to try to deal with the situation through explanation or badgering, I came to terms with the fact that Iya Dayo and I had a relationship that was rather different from the straightforward provision of translation services I had anticipated. Talking with women about money could not, I realised, be extricated from talk about relationships. And not just intimate relationships. Money featured in all manner of other relationships, including with God. Iya Dayo's relationship with God meant that she couldn't just be equanimous in these conversations. It was difficult for her not to speak, to share her views and to make herself heard. And it was difficult for me to insist that she hold back.

It was obvious that the presence of the field assistant might change the quality and nature of information an anthropologist was able to acquire. It just hadn't occurred to me that my assistant might block or distort the flow of information, consciously or unconsciously, overtly or covertly. It was as if the idea of a field assistant was to find someone who was a pale shadow of an actual human being with their own experiences, opinions, and values, who could simply relay rather than relate. But I had asked Iya Dayo what she thought we should study. I'd invited her into the research. And I'd done a very poor job of explaining exactly what it was that I expected of her.

It was a situation of my own making.

FEMINIST FABLES

As time went on, Iya Dayo and my differences gave layers of complexity to the research process that I came to value. We would have free-ranging conversations with women about work and money that would stray onto all manner of other topics, like love, infidelity, their husbands' failures to honour their part of the marital bargain and provide for their children, domestic violence, and the louche behaviour of the youth of today. Iya Dayo would have her own words to say about some of the things we were told, especially when it involved younger women and when the subject turned to their husbands. I could tell by the tone of her voice and her body language that she was conveying in Yoruba the moral views she'd voice in English when we were wandering back through Ilemi mulling over the day's interviews. Whenever I asked her to translate what she'd said, she'd give me short shrift.

Iya Dayo's disapproval of my curiosity about matters of love and romance was, arguably, outside her job description. But what I was asking of her was also beyond the topic we'd settled on at the outset. Sometimes she was reluctant to ask the questions I put to her to pass on, asking me why I wanted to know that or suggesting I might ask about something else. At others, she clearly did not want to convey to me what women said in response. On occasion, she would simply refuse to translate when the conversation turned bawdy or irreverent, folding her arms and tutting with disapproval. I knew from the interactions we had in English that she was fond of lecturing younger women about how they ought to obey their husbands and not complain. The condition of womanhood, she would tell them, was one of endurance.

All this did not sit well with my feminism. I started stepping outside the space of neutral curiosity and throwing in a few opinions of my own.

I realised that I had internalised a version of anthropology that treated what people told me as if they were actual facts that could be contaminated if gave my own view away. *Of course* I couldn't be neutral. My whiteness made it impossible. Iya Dayo's lectures about how it was women's duty to obey and endure was entirely consistent with the messages conveyed by the myriad churches, chapels, and other prayer venues in and around the town.

There was every reason for people to believe that even if I wasn't a missionary, I subscribed to the Christian mores that Iya Dayo was so keen to emphasise in her interventions. The problem was that it served to reinforce an implicit storyline about me with which I was deeply uncomfortable. And it made me complicit in something with which I disagreed very profoundly.

So I took to telling stories. I delved into my own lived experience and then ventured off into the realm of fiction, coming up with storylines that always elicited a response. I came to think of them as feminist fables, tales that had a purpose to their telling. These, I was later to discover, had an official term and a recognised place in qualitative research methodology. They were 'vignettes'.

Through the vignettes I would tell when people asked me about what women's lives were like in England, I positioned myself in a very different place to Iya Dayo. In some respects, I came to reflect later, her conservative views were the perfect foil. Our evident disagreement invited others in to share views that they may not have otherwise articulated. My vignettes caused other reactions: shock, sympathy, pity, disgust, disapproval.

When I was asked about marriage in Britain, my nearest point of reference was my mother and her friends. I didn't know any people my own age who were married. Marriage wasn't something I'd ever thought about doing myself. I associated it with loss: of freedom, of my name, of identity. If I'd been asked what being a married woman was like, I'd have come up with a picture of confinement and enforced domesticity - that's what I saw my mother go through. So to answer the questions about marriage, I turned to the vignettes she'd told me and started spinning tales from my childhood. Real stories, of women friends of my mother's who'd become feminist legends in the re-telling of how they'd navigated problematic husbands.

Like the one who'd cooked her husband a delicious meal and was sitting down with him to eat it, when she noticed him looking lasciviously at a young woman who was walking past their house, dressed in a short skirt. In a flash of fury, the friend had stood up, snatched the tablecloth in both of her hands and pulled it so sharply that food went flying in the air and down his front. I could picture him sitting there in bemused surprise, peas rolling down his sweater and gravy pooling in his crotch.

The retelling of this one brought howls of laughter. And then, "did he beat her after this?"

"I don't know," I said, "I don't think he was an especially violent man. He was just a leery old git."

I had to explain what leery old git meant, and we were laughing again. As we wiped the tears of our laughter away, the talk fell to more serious topics and the feminist fable did its work: breaking the ice, opening the space for a conversation that was more intimate than if I'd plunged in with my questions.

My favourite story was of a woman who called Betsy. The name conjured up in my imagination a wiry, short woman with auburn hair and a tweedy twin set, possibly also pearls, and a sensible brown handbag with matching brogues. These were details that I didn't share in my telling of the story of how Betsy taught her unfaithful husband a lesson. They would have meant little to my Nigerian listeners.

For me, talk of tweedy twin set, pearls and brogues does the very British thing of marking Betsy's likely age, race and class. Such is the British class system: once you learn its grammar, you can rattle off a string of associations that might in another context seem bizarrely specific, but which nail a particular class bracket with incredible accuracy. The handbag and shoes conjure up a visual picture that matches with that of someone who is almost definitely white, probably votes Tory, watches tennis but can't abide football. The kind of woman who makes batches of rich dark amber, thickly sliced, Seville marmalade every January, properly labelled with the date and stored in neat rows in the pantry to provide a supply for morning toast that lasts the year.

These, too, are the kind of details the anthropologist gathers.

Betsy had been a successful businesswoman in her own right. Something, if I remember rightly, to do with gems. I remembered opals, garnets, chunks of quartz. Perhaps she collected them. To me as a child they were jewels, objects associated with opulence. Whether she traded or acquired them through her business successes, Betsy was wealthy. Her husband was a drab shadow of a man. Let's call him Roger. He had thinning hair dressed in a comb-over and wore the kind of trousers that were called 'slacks' by people like Betsy and Roger. Their house was large, modern, expensively furnished. He drove the kind of car that matched her twin set, a sleek dark blue BMW saloon. He doubtless played golf and read *The Daily Telegraph*.

One night, or so the story my mother told me went, he pulled into their drive in his BMW. He got his briefcase from the passenger seat, reached into his trouser pocket for his keys and went to open the front door. His key wouldn't go in. He jabbed, poked and wiggled. Still no joy. He knocked on the door. No answer. Then he stepped over the low rose bushes that lined the drive to knock on the window in case his wife was somewhere else in the house. The light from the lamp in the street lit up the room inside. He gazed into it, uncomprehending. His lounge was entirely empty. The new three-piece suite with its gold dralon covers. The mahogany coffee table. The colour television that they'd just bought. The carriage clock that sat on the mantelpiece. All gone. He pressed his nose against the window, barely taking in what he saw.

When the police arrived, they, too, pressed their faces against the windows and tried the door. Then they tried the other doors of the house and, finally, made their way in through a window that had been left open. The house had been emptied. There was literally nothing left. Nothing, that is, apart from the man's shirts, suits, ties, and underpants. They remained where he'd left them early that morning, neatly arranged in an inbuilt wardrobe in a large, empty, upstairs bedroom. She'd taken the trouble of cutting off most of the arms of the suits and slashing the seams of the trousers before she left, and they dangled awkwardly in an otherwise orderly line.

This story brought shrieks. I told it slowly, with dramatic effect. "And when he found her, what then?", the women would ask, breathlessly. "He didn't," I said. "She'd packed out. He got a letter from her lawyers saying that she was suing him for divorce for infidelity and unreasonable conduct, and that the furniture was not the only thing that she'd be taking."

This would take us into lengthy discussions about when enough was enough, what women could do to ensure they had a backup plan so that if they needed to leave, they had somewhere to go. It surfaced, time and again, a sense amongst so many of the women I met that marriage was something to be endured, put up with, got on with. They weren't alone in this. Betsy was an exception amongst my mum's friends. Most of them, my mum included, endured. I'd hear them laughing their heads off, sharing stories like these. But when it came to it, most had no other option: they stayed put.

I could no more present a feminist rendition of empowered women in my own country than I could distinguish their options from those of the women I was talking with. It wasn't just about not having the means to support themselves. It was about a host of other things: respectability, family, reputation, security, stability, and the idea of giving children as idealised a childhood as possible, one that would not be disrupted by rupture. Theirs were also tales of resignation. Of getting on with life despite having been dealt a short hand when it came to the man they'd settled down with. Of making do. Women captured their pragmatism in a phrase that I heard repeated time and again: *face your children and your work.*

HAVING ISSUES

Soon I'd begun embellishing my stories, drawing them out in the telling for dramatic effect. Gasps and exclamations from my audiences egged me on. Before long, I was tearing a leaf out of my favourite Nigerian newspaper, that scurrilous repository of scandal and intrigue, *Lagos Weekend*, and turning news stories into true-life tales.

Wandering with Iya Dayo through the back streets of the quarter one afternoon, I'd called out a greeting to three men who were in their late middle age who were sitting in the shade of a long veranda. They beckoned us over, pulled out a couple of white plastic chairs and began questioning me in English.

Where was I from? What was I doing? Why had I come to Ilemi?

We ran through all the familiar questions. I proffered the well-rehearsed answers that by now came tumbling off my tongue.

We fell into a chat about the current state of morality in Nigeria, prompted by a story told by one of the men about one of the smuggler boys they called *fayawo*. That lad, he told us, had stashed his jerrycans of smuggled petrol in the house of his girlfriend. She was the wife of a chief. He had so many wives, that man, and rumour had it he wasn't able to give any of them children. So, the wives had to find another way to get themselves established.

Something I learnt early on about marriage in Ilemi was that without what people called *issue* – children – it was incredibly hard to secure a marriage. I'd always seen marriage as a state or a status. Ideally one to be avoided. I came to understand it as a process of acquiring and accumulating entitlements, with recognisable landmarks along the way. Betrothal and marriage ceremonies were ritual moments, in a similar way to the role of weddings in Britain. But the making of marriages was less the kind of 'work' spoken about in relation to companionate marriage in Britain than the creation of a familial bond and associated obligations through 'having issue'. Without children, it was difficult to sustain a marriage for long. Or for women to remain in their relationships free of a second or third wife.

Pregnancy marked the start of many marriages. It was the point at which relationships solidified into something longer lasting. I'd heard stories circulating about young women getting pregnant and being accused of trying to 'pin' the pregnancy on an 'owner' who could give them the best possible arrangements in which to bring up the children. Iya Dayo used to specialise in these kinds of cautionary tales, featuring young women who *uselessed themselves* by having lots of lovers and then ended up being unable to work out who was the real 'owner' of their pregnancy.

After all, women told me, once you have a child with someone, you're connected with them. As long as there's a child between you, there will be an entire lifetime of obligation ahead of you. But if you don't bear a child or that child becomes ill and dies, your relationship becomes so brittle it can easily break.

"That man kept on marrying wives, so he'd be able to find one who could bear issue for him. The first wife had no issue. The second wife had no issue. That third wife was a new one, and that's where the trouble started."

"But what if it was him?" I asked, interrupting the story.

"What if he was the one who was infertile?"

The men all laughed. That was impossible! The man was a chief. He'd just been unlucky with the wives. But then one of the men began to tell another tale of a woman in the neighbouring compound who had become pregnant after more than a decade of marriage.

The husband loved her very much. He'd steadfastly resisted his mother's persistent efforts to get him to take a second wife. More than ten years passed. By the time, the whole family were on his case. She'd gone from the Muslim *alfa* at the end of the street, who had her drinking verses from the Koran written on bits of paper and soaked to make a spiritual tonic, to attending the prayer sessions at one of the new Pentecostal churches, where the priest's flashy Mercedes was taken as proof of the power of his prayerfulness. She'd even secretly paid a visit to an herbalist, who'd given her an oily, dense black substance to smear on her private parts, claiming that it would facilitate pregnancy.

All of this came to nothing. Every month, she'd see blood and her hopes would be dashed.

Then, he said, she became pregnant. As her belly swelled, people began to comment. It had been a long time. Her husband had been so good to her, not sending her back to her father's house or taking another wife. But when that child was born it did not look anything like him.

"*Omo ale!*", one of the other men shouted, "it be so!"

It turned out that she had become tired of waiting. Her husband had a driver.

"She got that man to give her the pregnancy".

Omo ale literally means 'child of the evening'; the one born from the sneaking around needed to do the necessary. There were all kinds of things to say about *omo ale*. A popular tale involved the child growing up to be the spitting image of the biological father, a daily reminder.

"Those children, they never get anywhere in life," said one.

"They're the ones who succeed," said another.

Everyone, it turned out, had a view. Their views were divergent enough to keep us in lively conversation for half an hour or more.

One of the men turned to me, "what about in your country?".

"It's easier than that," I said. "You can just go and buy yourself some sperm."

They gasped with shock and looked at me in disbelief.

I told them of a case that had made the newspapers just before I left, a clinic that supplied lesbians with sperm. The men were agog. It was a lot to take in. Buying sperm. Women being able to just go and buy themselves a pregnancy, without a husband.

Iya Dayo sat stiffly, her lips pursed.

And what, they asked, was a lesbian? I set about explaining.

"Lesbians are women who have sex with women."

"How now?" one of the men exclaimed.

Iya Dayo shot me a warning look. It was getting to the point where she might just put her foot down and refuse to translate. I reined myself back in.

"Time for us to go," I beamed at Iya Dayo. We said our goodbyes and took the winding path through the quarter back to the market.

TROUBLING CULTURE

I was schooled to be a social anthropologist, a kind of anthropologist who studies the social world. Social anthropology originated in the idea that an anthropologist can, through fieldwork, discover the rules, structures and systems through which societies organise the most important things in life: having children, making a living, belonging, staying alive. What I was grappling with when people asked me about how people do things in my country was, in essence, what anthropologists recognise by the word 'culture'. It's a loose term with a lot of different meanings. The British social anthropologist Edmund Tylor famously defined it in 1871 as 'that complex whole which includes knowledge, belief, art, morals, law, custom, and any other capabilities and habits acquired by man as a member of society'.

The problems with thinking about culture in the singular as 'that complex whole' weren't just academic. Reading Raymond Williams, Stuart Hall, Cornel West, and other icons of Cultural Studies had made me aware of cultures within cultures, the intimate relationship between culture, race, and class, and the trouble with any attempt to define a single Culture.

If the origin myths of the town were to be believed, the town was founded by strangers: no-one was originally there. In one of those myths, in a book I'd found in SOAS library published by colonial anthropologist A.B. Ellis in 1894 called *The Yoruba-Speaking Peoples of the Slave Coast*, Ilemi sprung up on the site in a forest clearing where the creator goddess Odudua had ravished a handsome young hunter who she'd taken a fancy to as she travelled through the place. I liked the sound of that. A goddess slaking her thirst for pleasure in a verdant paradise was a fine way to begin, as origins go.

Awori Yoruba claimed the town as theirs because they got there first. Was their version of 'Yoruba culture' the one I should be studying, if I was to study 'The Yoruba'? Egbado Yoruba had found sanctuary in Ilemi, escaping the internecine wars of the nineteenth century. They'd run away from those who would sell them into slavery, head-loading their possessions barefoot to reach safety and found themselves behind the long, high, wall that surrounded the town and kept her people safe from predators. And they'd stayed, farming lands around the town, building houses in quarters of the town that were to be named by the ethnicity of those who'd settled there.

Ijebus and Ileshas and other Yoruba migrants from Ogbomosho, Ilorin and further north had come to take advantage of opportunities as the town expanded in the 1920s and 1930s to become a lively trading post. Other Yoruba from further north still had migrated south looking for opportunities and settled. While Ado was very much a Yoruba town in its sense of itself and its identity, among the townsfolk were Egun people who farmed lands and came from hamlets to the west of the town as well as Igbo, Hausa, Ibibio and others from across the country and beyond its borders, from Ghana, Benin and Togo.

From what I'd gathered up to that point, the habits, outlooks and traditions of all of these different groups couldn't be neatly classified as 'Yoruba'. They were different from each other. Perhaps I could enquire into this, I wondered, tracing the different ethnic groups and the way in which the subtle differences between them when it came to marriage and divorce, women's work, birthing, naming and child-rearing.

In the end, I started where the traditional anthropologist might seek to begin. Iya Dayo and I spent hours interviewing elderly men and trying to work out a kinship diagram of the Awori Yoruba family from whom claims to kingship of this little town came. I gathered the list of names. I drew circles and triangles, the branches and the stems. It was all neatly laid out on a large sheet of blue paper. I'd then folded the paper and put it on the bottom shelf of the storage unit in the corner of my room.

The rats had started at the edges and nibbled in, with one or two of them taking large bits out of the centre and along the lines where the paper folded, causing the whole thing to fall apart in my hands when I discovered it. I'd sat there on the floor of my room weeping tears of frustration whilst I tried to piece together again the elaborate - and ultimately completely pointless - performance of proper anthropologist that the diagram had represented. I never did manage to reconstruct it.

Luckily, I never found myself in need of any such thing.

Many years later, I was to blush when having proudly handed around my fieldnote books for students to look at what a real anthropologist does, I saw one begin to giggle as they read. I went over to find out what was so funny. "Fucking rats ate my kinship diagram," the entry began.

Kinship was not just a matter for the anthropologist's curiosity. The line of descent had been contested and there was currently no king in the town. The dispute between the family had been raging for many years. Yoruba towns and their governance arrangements had foxed the colonials, who couldn't grasp why in some towns there was more than one king. Famously, in nearby Abeokuta, the British exercised the kind of crushing colonial stupidity familiar to colonised peoples across Africa and beyond. They just picked one of the kings to recognise as the legitimate ruler of the town, with whom they'd try to strike their political bargains, and left out the rest.

As for the queens, as elsewhere in Africa, they got short shrift from the colonisers. For all the esteem in which the British people held their own Queen Victoria, Yoruba queens got none of that recognition. But the colonial administration got what they deserved when the women of Aba mobilised to push back on their taxes and stood facing the shameful colonials stark naked. And the legendary Funmilayo Ransome-Kuti, mother of musician Fela Kuti, who was described as the "Lioness of Lisabi" for her organising powers, mobilised thousands of women, leading a wave of protests demanding an end to unfair taxes for market women.

Was colonial social anthropology so preoccupied with kinship, I wondered, because it was ultimately about understanding who had access to power and resources? Who was related to whom mattered when you were trying to create an empire, especially using the techniques mastered by the British: double-dealing, duplicity, divide-and-rule. The applied anthropologists of the colonial period included some of the discipline's most influential figures. They specialised not just in kinship, but also in understanding the architectures of rule. Many contributed to shaping the engagement of the colonial authorities with the governance of the territories in which they studied precisely through decoding and describing how people were related.

People's accounts of 'how things are done here' were at best rather unreliable, because of their desire to represent to the ever-curious anthropologist a version that would fit the world the anthropologist might be coming from themselves. I quickly began to recognise that this was especially the case when it came to the basic elements of kinship: the formation of families through marriage and reproduction.

I knew from the reading I'd done before my trip that the rules of relatedness weren't altogether straightforward in this part of Nigeria. Some people traced their genealogy strictly through the father's line in what was called *agnatic kinship*. Others were more flexible and, it was hinted, opportunistic, in their choices of tracing connections through either their mother's or their father's line. This was known as *cognatic kinship*. Mastery of these technical details was part of the training I received as an undergraduate. At the time, I'd seen kinship as dry and boring. I hadn't quite seen the potential in it. Kinship wasn't only about the rules of relatedness. It was about relationships. If I'd been able to reframe it in my mind and realise that all that word 'kinship' meant was how people got to be related, I'd have clocked that it involves sex and love and intimacy, abortion and infertility, broken hearts, affairs, family pressures to tie the knot, years of bleak endurance and then, finally, a room of one's own.

At that stage, though, I hadn't quite got there yet. I was still struggling to work out what it was that I was doing in Ilemi. My curiosity led me down so many paths that I felt as if I was lost in a maze, going this way and that trying to find my way out.

WE PAGANS

Something had to happen. I'd set off for Lagos on my own, against everyone's advice. I found it hard to confess that sometimes I needed a little time to myself. But that's what this was all about. And there was no better a place to find the peace I craved than in the chaos and energy of Lagos. Surfing the lanes of the Third Mainland Bridge after crawling through the thick treacle of traffic all the way from Ota was exhilarating. Drivers attempting to overtake – and they did, constantly, on the inside and outside, and sometimes both simultaneously - would get ahead and then look in their mirrors to see a white woman driving her own car, and it would almost make them swerve right into the next audacious overtaking vehicle.

It made me feel full of my own power. I'd taken to it as a habit that was proving a little too addictive for Grace's liking.

"Take Tade with you", Grace would say. "Let Dapo drive you. Lagos is a bad place-o. It's not good for you to keep going there alone."

"Never mind," I would retort. "I can look after myself. In any case, Tade has to go to school and where would Dapo sleep?"

Rumour had it that I had a lover in Lagos. Why else would I keep slipping off there at any opportunity? And why else would I want to go there alone?

That morning before setting off, I'd feasted on boiled yam and the delicious scotch bonnet pepper and tomato sauce that Grace made to go with it. As usual, I took the Ota road, weaving adeptly through the potholes and using my horn to overtake the rusty *danfo* that plied the route between Ota and Ilemi, racing past small hamlets and lush green fields spotted with palm trees before joining the fray at Ota. When Stanley and I first set out on our travels, I was soon to recognise that my reserved English driving style, with its copious use of the indicator, was more hazardous than acquiring brash new ways of the road from those around me.

The sprawling market at the intersection with the Abeokuta-Lagos road reminded me of the tale told to me the week before by one of my market women friends I concerned a cloth seller who had a lover in Ota, a lover in Lagos and a husband at home. By all accounts, she'd got herself the kind of magical medicine that makes men forget, *oogun iyonu*. In any case, the husband didn't suspect anything. He was happy enough that she was earning so much from her trade that he didn't need to spend any of his own money on the children's schooling or food. But one day, she narrowly avoided meeting her undoing.

She'd gone to Ota for the market, having lined up a little extracurricular activity for the sleepy time in the mid-afternoon when the sun is so hot, and everyone is so sluggish that there is barely any point sweltering in the market with hardly a customer in sight. That day, or so rumour had it, she went as usual to the place where her lover had found them a room and waited for him there. But then she'd heard voices outside the door. She realised to her horror that her sister-in-law and her husband were standing there in the courtyard outside her room. She had kicked the door shut with her foot and sat there anxiously willing them to leave before her lover – a large, effusive man whose roars of laughter would wake a sleeping baby – arrived. There would be no pretending, no defending herself: this was the kind of place people went for an hour or so of fun. The minutes ticked by. My market woman friend laughed as she told me. She had to wait there. She could hear everything they were saying. Then, finally, they left.

I couldn't imagine how these women got away with it. I admired their guts: if they got caught in the act, they'd face all kinds of trouble. Some would be beaten. Others would be sent back to their father's house. Men had no such constraint. I'd hear stories from women about having suffered the indignity of the husband bringing home another wife, and parading her in front of them, showing them who's boss. A neighbour, Bola, had told me of how her husband's family never liked her much, so when he brought a new wife home, they made a big fuss of their *iyawo* – the new wife. He'd brought that wife to sleep in their room, in their bed, making Bola sleep on a mat on the floor beside them. And, she said, there was nothing she could do.

"That's why a woman needs her own money," she'd said, "so she can pack out when the husband starts misbehaving. She needs it so she can build her own house, and then the husband can come and visit her there. Then she won't have to suffer."

I turned my attention back to the road. The traffic had snarled up. I spent the next hour crawling forward in the dense smog of traffic fumes, cut up to the left and the right by impatient *danfos*.

My trips to Lagos always involved a visit to the anonymous looking office by the taxi motor park where I'd exchange a single hundred-dollar bill for a brown paper bag full of Naira. As the months went on, I'd extract the notes from my lucky wrapper, one by one, and cash them in. The thick wad of Naira I'd bring back would go to Grace and Iya Dayo, and then be divided up into small bundles and planted artfully around my room, stashed in letters, filed in books, stuffed in socks.

When I settled in Ilemi, one of the first things I did was to go to the bank on the high street to open an account. It was unusually quiet inside. No queues. No customers. A clerk offered me a laconic grin as I entered.

"Madam, you can sit here," he gestured to an empty row of plastic chairs, before disappearing.

After some while, the door marked MANAGER with the big gold-edged sign opened. A large man emerged, resplendent in a spotless white lace *agbada* matched with white lace trousers and a cap. He laughed a loud, long belly laugh when I said I wanted to open an account. I experienced one of those clanging moments of Britishness, when something that seemed perfectly sensible, routine even, melts into being somehow inexplicably ridiculous without ever really understanding why.

And so it was with my bank account.

The manager dutifully opened the account. I dutifully signed the papers, deposited a small quantity of Naira and walked home, passbook in hand, a little bemused. The next time I went there, they were out of money. And the next. I began to see why people had found my desire for a bank account so entertaining.

Everyone I knew used the collectors who visited their clients daily to scoop up the day's proceeds and keep them safe for a small fee. I was struck by this, pointing out that where I came from banks paid people interest to keep their money, rather than levying a charge. But I soon came to understand the economic logic of the daily collection that people called *ajo*. Market traders are relieved of the day's takings before their children descended on them, returning home with no spare cash for husbands or in-laws to 'borrow'. Even those who turn a considerable profit were happy enough to hand a day's worth over each month just to be prevented from having any spare cash to spend.

I casually lodged my brown paper bag full of Naira in the boot, as if it were a bag of potatoes, and dislodged Stanley from the clutches of the parking tout. I wished that the business of having the bank account had worked out, and there were some other means of guaranteeing a safe passage for my cash than carrying it myself from Lagos. But Stanley's bowels provided a safe enough repository, at least for now.

With a gentle purr, we set off on the journey back to Ilemi. Cars jostled bumper to bumper on the flyovers, touts pressing pirated videos and lurid magazines through the window in the stretches of go-slow. The rank stench of road filled the air. Dusk was only a couple of hours away, and even I was not foolish enough not to get back home before night fell.

A couple of miles from Ota, I spotted a side road that I'd never noticed before. It gleamed with newly laid asphalt. A short cut. Without thinking through the possible implications, including the possibility that the road did not, after all, go anywhere near Ilemi, I took it. Stanley glided delightedly along the newly paved road. It did not have a single pothole. Road-building contracts were a notorious source of illicit lucre. Kickbacks to contractors were legion. And many new road surfaces disintegrated within months of being completed. The roads around Ilemi were pocked with the results. But this one, for now, was perfection itself. Stanley had just had his carburettor tuned and was purring obligingly. So smooth was the road that he leapt forward with a gentle roar.

Stanley and I cruised along companionably. Gentle undulating slopes covered in oil palm plantations lined the road, the trees casting a long shadow in the late afternoon sun. The route was peppered with sparse settlements, the landscape broken up with the occasional smatter of mud plaster houses, with their rusting corrugated roofs. Suddenly the peace was abruptly shattered. A large wrenching clunk rang out. The car came to a sudden halt. It felt as if Stanley's guts had fallen out. I opened the door, half expecting to see a dark stain oozing out from underneath the chassis onto the glistening black asphalt. Instead, there was a large, rusty, lump of metal. It looked like the exhaust had come off in one piece. I stood there for a while, stunned.

I took stock of the situation. The light had begun to fade. There I was, standing in the middle of an empty road in the middle of the bush with a disembowelled car. The crushing weight of the cautionary tales used to remonstrate with me in vain efforts to make me see the folly of my ways suddenly caught up with me. I was alone in the bush, at the mercy of armed robbers. And worse. There weren't even *danfos* plying this route. I'd barely seen another vehicle.

"*Oyinbo!*"

A shrill cry rang through the air. Two small boys ran towards me, followed by another, smaller, child.

"*Oyinbo! Oyinbo!*"

Following the children was a short man, wearing a tattered red polo shirt and stained jeans. It took me a couple of seconds to recognise traces of engine oil on his trousers, and to realise my luck. It was a mechanic. I'd heard tales of people breaking down in the bush and mechanics emerging from nowhere, but I had always thought they were wishful myths. But here he was, flesh and blood, coming towards me with a broad smile all over his face.

"How body?" he asked.

"Fine, fine," I said, "but my car is not." I pointed to the rusted deposit that lay beneath the car.

Flinging himself onto the ground, he slid under the car. Emerging a few seconds later, he told me that it wasn't serious. The exhaust system had fallen off, he would call his boys and they would push the car off the road. It wouldn't take long to mend.

I could have hugged him. I desisted, as by now a crowd of small boys had begun to gather, intrigued to see an *oyinbo* at close range.

A couple of the boys pulled the exhaust system out from under the car and pulled it in the direction of the small cluster of mud plaster and corrugated roof houses that sat at the crest of the hill. The mechanic took the wheel and steered Stanley gently towards the edge of the road. I joined his open-mouthed assistants taking up the rear, as we guided the car onto a patch of flattened earth close to a crumbling whitewashed building with a faded cross perched on its crown.

The mechanic rolled up his sleeves, tugged the exhaust back under the car then dived under the chassis and set to work. The children stood at some distance from us, as if fearful of the woman with the strange blue eyes and pink skin. As I began to chat with the mechanic, they drew near, transfixed.

The creaking doors of the church sprang open. A man in a long cassock emerged, bespectacled and grey haired. He approached me with warm familiarity, as if we knew each other, and shook my hand enthusiastically.

"Sister!" he said. He meant Sister as in Catholic. It seemed inevitable that he would mistake me for a nun. I was tired and stressed about getting home. Being appropriated like this by the priest really irritated me.

"I'm not a Sister," I retorted, "I'm an...," I grappled for what to substitute Sister with, "... an Anthropologist." Somewhat gratuitously, I also threw in, "and I'm not a Christian".

The children gasped and drew closer. The man in the cassock drew himself up to his full height and eyed me suspiciously.

"What do you mean, you are not a Christian? You're white. It's your people who brought us Christianity."

"I know," I said. "But in my country, there are many people who aren't Christians."

"In fact," I added, "most people aren't Christians. Very few people go to church these days."

"If you're not a Christian, what are you then?" he asked me, with a tone that was almost accusatory, as if I were lying for effect.

I thought for a minute. My professions of atheism often ended up in lengthy discussions that all too often lapsed into heavy-handed attempts at conversion.

I tried a different tack.

"I'm a pagan."

There was stunned silence. The young lads began to giggle, nervously.

"A pagan?" He rolled the words thickly off his tongue, pronouncing every syllable. P-AG-AN.

"Yes," I smiled sweetly.

I moved to close the conversation there and then. I'd had too many of those protracted enquiries into my beliefs, or lack thereof.

"It was a pleasure to meet you, Sir. And now let me attend to my vehicle."

"A pagan?" he said again. He looked utterly bewildered.

"Do they have pagans in your country?"

"Oh yes," I said. "We have a lot of pagans. Some believe in the power of witchcraft. They call it Wicca."

He let out an audible gasp. And then, abruptly, he took his leave. He turned on his heel and went back into the church, crossing himself surreptitiously as he crossed the threshold and pulling the doors to with a clank.

The mechanic, who had been listening to the exchange from under the car, wriggled out and jumped to his feet.

He had a wide grin on his face.

"Madam, it is fixed."

I thanked him, dipping into my bra like a market woman and pulling out a thick wad of Naira, which I pressed into his hand.

Just in time. The light was fast fading.

"How far is it to Ilemi?" I asked nervously, preoccupied with the possibility that the make-shift repair might not last the journey.

"I'll drive you," he said.

"That's so kind of you, but how will you get back?"

"I'll get an *ocada*", he said, referring to the swarm of small motorbikes that massed around Ilemi's market area at dusk. I nodded, smiling my thanks.

As we drove towards Ilemi, the luscious landscape around us bathed with the red-gold glow of the setting sun, he turned to me.

"Christians stick together. Muslims stick together. We pagans, we need to stick together too."

'IN MY CULTURE'

Anthropologists rarely report on the questions they get asked by their informants. But I wasn't the only one, I was to discover, who got to exercise their curiosity. There's an understanding amongst anthropologists that the first bit of your fieldwork is when you'll be most alert to cultural difference. You should make the most of it and take yourself on a steep learning curve, writing copious notes and asking questions along the way.

The same thing could be said for the people amongst whom anthropologists have decided to plant themselves for the purpose of study. At the beginning of their fieldwork, the anthropologist is strange, and their habits, customs, and ways of doing things might be similarly subject to inspection and inquiry. I'd often be called over and asked questions about what white people did and about life in the UK, as well as about myself and what I was doing there. And when I carried out more formal interviews, I'd ask the standard interviewer's final question, "is there anything you'd like to ask me?" and then the interview would begin in earnest.

The questions I was constantly asked about "in your country" were as anthropological as it comes. The challenge was how to answer them.

Curious snippets about Britain and its public figures made it into the Nigerian newspapers. The Royal Family were held in fascination. They were often the subject of questions, not least because of the scandals rocking the Monarchy at the time. *Lagos Weekend* and *Intimate Affairs* hadn't been slow to pick up on Prince Charles' tampon chat. People wanted to know what the

Queen thought of it all.

British politics was also often a topic, especially amongst the elderly men who'd retired to Ilemi after long years in white collar careers that began as clerks during the colonial period Margaret Thatcher was held in some admiration by some. For others, she was regarded as the very epitome of the mentality of colonial Britain. There was something too-powerful about her that was placed in contrast with the Queen, who was always pictured smiling and shaking hands but never saying anything much. When I told people I'd originally been drawn to Nigeria because of what I read about women and power, they'd refer me back to Margaret Thatcher and the Queen and say, "but in your country you have women in charge."

Anthropology is a discipline founded on comparison. Early anthropologists were preoccupied by discovering systems of social rules that could be contrasted across different cultures. That's where all that interest in kinship was directed: at establishing rules and working out whether they applied in different places, to establish a kind of grammar of relatedness. So dominant was the influence of a handful of British white male anthropologists, I read one article that made the case that African kinship systems – yes, all 54 African states could be reduced to a single country even by an anthropologist – didn't apply to the New Guinea highlands.[3]

How could I describe 'British culture' when people asked me about how things were in my country? The assumption was that in my country things would be different, rather than the same. The very question "how about in your country?" invited me to provide a contrast. Anthropologists were good at this. Aspects of other cultures were given names in the vernacular, italicised, and described as if they were beguiling instances of something completely different. I could easily supply completely different, proving them right. But this was, I came to realise, a choice. I could be lazy and reach for a stereotype. Or I could draw on my own experience in all its messy complexity and find commonalities that they might not have been expecting at all.

Much of what an anthropologist would consider to be 'culture' can be found in the everyday things that we might not be particularly aware of doing and might be hard pressed to regard as worth explaining. To give an account of *our culture*, we need to be able to find things that seem to be distinctive to us as a cultural group. This calls for us to create something of a cultural identity, in order to explain it. There's a brilliant book by anthropologist Kate Fox called *Watching the English* that includes chapters on weather talk, shopping at M&S and garden centres – examples of a kind of constructed Englishness that English people might instantly identify once they'd been pointed out to them. That's the point. They're constructed. And they need to be pointed out.

I'd also come to associate the idea of *our culture* as a way in which white British people distance themselves from practices associated with people from another place. The term carries with it an undercurrent of faintly voiced disparagement or disapproval, voiced in a tone that carries a very British sense of superiority; they'd say, *"it's their culture,"* to bring attention to someone doing something differently to the way *they* would do it. "It's their culture" translates as "those odd things that those people do that aren't how we do things round here." *Their* Culture is not *Our* Culture. *It's their culture* preserves a mentality that keeps our little island smug and separate.

I'd heard *"it's their culture"* a lot as a child visiting my white working-class grandparents in a part of Birmingham called Handsworth in the late 1960s and early 1970s. I learnt to associate it with something harsher and more disquieting: racism. The first thing I got to know about the existence of other cultures was from grandparents complaining of how the odour of curry lingered in the air as they tended to the roses in their little back garden.

My grandparents had been moved from the bomb-stricken tenements of the inner city to one of the shiny new council houses built in Handsworth after the war. It was a time of hardship, but also of hope. A new Labour government was putting the Welfare State in place, rebuilding the wreckage of a country emerging from the privations of the second world war. My father recalls the wonderment with which he ate his first banana, a fruit he'd never seen before. The boats that brought bananas also carried a precious cargo of people who came to assist Britain's reconstruction. They came to settle in areas like Handsworth, bringing a wider world to the white working-class neighbourhood.

It must have been some time in the late 1960s that I first saw a Black person. They were walking down the street in Handsworth as my father drove my mother and sisters in our Morris Traveller to visit my father's family. My auntie had married the man she first went out with at the age of 14, whose family lived nearby. My uncle's wife's family lived on the other side of the road. Horizons were limited.

My grandma kept cupcakes with candied cherries and white icing in a tin in the pantry. As a child, I'd be sent down there in the morning to fetch the tin with biscuits in, which my sisters and I would dunk in our tea as we sat giggling with my grandma in her bed. We'd eat our meals in a room that was used only for that purpose, with a large dark wood table and placemats featuring paintings of rural scenes. I came across similar customs amongst Zimbabwe's white farmers many years later, frozen in white British culture from the 1930s.

I'd grown up calling Europe *the Continent*. It was a place described in terms that had the effect of applauding whatever national characteristic of the British used to make the contrast. The dirty French. The lazy Spanish. The humourless Germans. For all my ability to laugh, I happened to be a child of one of those Germans. On both sides of my family, there was a foreignness that would never be resolved, my foreign mother never fully assimilated in his country, my foreign father never fully accepted in hers. *It's their culture* was never verbalised to account for the thin seam of difference that ran through everything in my family, but we felt it all the same.

These days, those who apply for British citizenship have to be put through a test that involves a series of questions about what is euphemistically called 'British traditions and customs'. It costs £50 and the government website takes you to a privatised service touting e-learning and textbooks that become essential if you want to pass the test. No such resources were available to me as I grappled to respond to questions in Ilemi about how we did things in my culture. Even if I had, I am not sure how useful the correct answers to the citizenship quiz would be in describing the ways of my people to curious Nigerians who asked me to tell them things about my country.

I didn't know how many players there were in a cricket team. I'd never learnt the order of England's monarchs and couldn't tell them apart, except the man the British curiously celebrate for murder and infidelity, Henry VIII, and Elizabeth I - there were so few queens, each of them was special. I didn't know how long ago it was that Queen Boadicea roamed the land, although I had a vivid picture of her in my imagination from a book that I'd once read, defying assumptions about what it meant to be female. I couldn't name a single character from the radio soap opera The Archer.

I wouldn't pass the British citizenship test, that's for sure. But what exactly was it testing? What kind of Britishness did those questions assert? I struggled to find the things that defined *my culture*.

Then I thought again. Perhaps I was starting in the wrong place. I thought about how this idealised idea of British culture applied to real people. Where would I look to find examples of it? Could I identify people who were exemplars of Britishness, and describe them? Should I paint a picture from what I saw on TV? What about scenes from my everyday life, as a British person. Or from my family? Or should I choose examples from amongst my friends? They were hardly representative of mainstream British Culture in any shape or form, but I'd much rather have claimed theirs as *my culture* than the other options available to me.

I'd been socialised in settings more varied than many British people would be exposed to as children, from the aristocracy of the feudal north-east to the chattering classes in genteel southern England, from council houses to cul-de-sacs. I'd seen a lot of British cultures. Which version would I draw on in telling people about where I was from?

Of all my relatives, my mother was arguably the most astute observer of British Culture because she'd spent decades trying to assimilate into it. Culture with a capital C played into this. The French sociologist Pierre Bourdieu came up with the term 'cultural capital'. If you had lots of it, you were rich with references to works of art, galleries, symphonies, dinner party small talk, intelligent witticisms. Cultural capital gave you an unearned pot of resources for being in the right class, which could be spent to gain privileges.

My mother used her foreignness to float across the strictures of the British class system, to accumulate and seek to use as much cultural capital as she could get her hands on. For all of her efforts, she remained stubbornly difficult to place within the elaborate categorisation of class that British people carry in their heads. Her Anglicised German had a mix of code words in it that could identify her with any number of possible groupings. She'd taken, for example, to referring to the upstairs 'lounge', a word used by the middle and lower classes, as a 'drawing room'. It was a pretention that failed to match the room itself, but that gave her an account of herself that evoked the grandeur of a country pile or elegant town house. She'd sometimes refer to things as 'classy', meaning 'associated with upper classes': a term that virtually no-one in those classes would ever use.

I thought of my father's relatives. They were as traditional English as it gets. They didn't have much cultural capital to hand. My grandad wouldn't eat anything with any herbs or spices in it, and refused pasta, rice and everything that sounded or looked 'foreign'. They had the traditional English food known as 'meat and two veg' for their tea – a leathery slice of beef or pork or chicken, served with potato and a green vegetable like peas or cabbage that would be boiled until soft and watery and bathed in an unctuous salty brown gravy made from granules kept in a jar in the pantry. The main dish was followed by a cake-like sweet dish or canned fruit with little chunks of pineapple and pear and a bright red cherry, served with a dollop of ice cream. This was called 'sweet'. Or, if we were feeling fancy, 'dessert'. Posh people called it 'pudding'.

Should I describe this as my culture? When people asked what people eat in my country, what kind of people should I tell them about? I'd grown up on pasta, quick and easy to prepare for a mother of four children who'd gone back to college to get a degree. I'd eaten more Spaghetti Bolognese than I'd had hot dinners of the kind we served my grandparents when they came to visit. My diet reflected London's many cultures and communities. I ate pots of tangy light pink taramasalata from the corner shop across the road in Tufnell Park, tearing off chunks of delicious Cypriot bread to dip in it. I'd order take-away Chinese and Indian meals for a treat. The nearest I got to English food was the occasional bacon sandwich. So, what exactly was "my culture"?

There is in this a fundamental challenge for anthropologists. There's been much ink spilled on it. But the focus has largely been on cultural *difference* rather than the commonalities between us as human beings. Distinctions that show distinctiveness. Comparisons that highlight contrasts. Anthropology finds its fascination in the things we don't have in common. But something that struck me as I tried to find an adequate way of conveying "my culture" was that in any number of respects, we weren't actually that different at all. Sure, it sometimes took a stretch of the imagination to see those commonalities. And I would be a poor student not to be able to identify some fairly significant differences. But you could go through any number of things and find that when it came down to it, people are not that different to each other. Rather than looking for difference, I started noticing the commonalities, drawing parallels, looking not for evidence of otherness or sameness but in appreciation of our shared humanity. And this brought an empathy to my enquiries that I'd come to feel that anthropology somehow lacks. By making things strange in order to analyse them, people's lived experience ends up being sublimated to the intellectual project of interpretation.

Quite a few of the things people did in Ado could be dressed up in anthropological parlance. But once I saw them through a more empathetic lens, they were pretty much like what people did around me when I lived in London. When people were exhausted and felt aches and pains, for example, they'd think there was a sickness coming on and they'd doff a cocktail of pills to pre-empt it. I could give the pills their collective local name, *onisemejo*. I could reflect anthropologically on illness behaviour and on understandings of causation. One of my flatmates in London had a habit of doing the same. As soon as he felt a sniff coming on, he'd take a handful of pills, with zinc, Vitamin C and a paracetamol amongst them. *Onisemejo.*

At its worst, anthropological comparison sustains the lies that permit people from my culture to regard themselves as superior to others. I recall my puzzlement at the way one of the celebrated anthropologists in my department bracketed his own Christianity off from his analysis of West African religious beliefs and practices, explaining it to me once as part of an elaborate distinction between the rational and the irrational. I wasn't cheeky enough to comment that practices such as the ritual consumption of a dry wafer and mouthful of wine being described as the body and blood of a man who had died many centuries earlier seemed to me to stray into a zone not a million miles away from commissioning a *babalawo* to sacrifice a chicken to ward off those with malevolent intentions causing havoc in your life and eating it in a stew, as I had once done in Ibadan.

I couldn't honestly see much difference between going to a church to utter prayers for things you desired or to request divine intervention in preventing misfortune, commissioning the herbalist to sacrifice an animal to ward off malevolent spirits or swallowing verses from the Qur'an as prescribed by the Muslim healers called *alfa*. Essentially all of this was about the ways in which people cope with uncertainty, deferring to a power of some kind to help get them through. I did not know a single British person who observed no protective rituals at all, whether it involves avoiding walking under ladders, throwing spilled salt over your left shoulder, or not tempting fate by uttering fearful thoughts about something bad that might happen.

For those of all religions and none, these little ritual acts give us a feeling that we can do something to make our worlds safer. It is something that we share across cultures. It is what makes us human.

BLAMED FOR BAKASSI

Stanley swung onto the Badagry Expressway, joining the jumble of Lagos-bound traffic. I could see what Nigerians called a 'go-slow' ahead. Grace and Margaret had decided the night before that they would accompany me to Lagos. Within a few minutes, we were snarled up in the traffic jam. It stretched far into the horizon. We crawled along, flanked on both sides by impatient drivers seeking to insert their vehicles into whatever stream of traffic seemed to be moving slightly faster, hooting furiously. Cars strode what pavement there was by the side of the road to edge their way forward and wedged their way into any gaps that opened up. It was chaos.

Touts wandered through the jammed lanes calling for custom and pressing their wares. Flies flocked in through the half-opened window, resisting our attempts to chase them away. Dense fumes mingled in with the smells of warm asphalt and the mounds of burning waste by the side of the road choked us. Not for us the land cruisers of the development set, nor the air-conditioned Mercedes Benz of Ilemi's big men and women. Stanley's carpeted seats were the only residue of his former grandeur, and little help to us in this sweltering heat.

Stanley was now adorned with two of the finest car stickers a little stall in one of the big mainland Lagos markets had to offer. *Devil Keep Out! My Life is a Dangerous Zone!* one of them warned. *No Condition is Permanent*, reassured the other. I'd been looking out for *Horn before Overtaking*. But they'd run out. The vendor could only offer me *Angels on Guard*, which I politely refused. Not that anyone needed any encouragement to use their horn. It was one of the Nigerian driving habits I took back with me to London.

Suddenly, there was a clearing in the traffic. Into it stepped a soldier in green fatigues with a black-edged beret. He swayed and belched as he pointed his rifle at Stanley and gestured us to a halt.

"Get out," he spat, jabbing the air with his rifle. "Get OUT".

I timidly opened the door and stepped onto the steaming asphalt, smoothing down my dress. I was thankful that I'd followed Grace's instructions and worn a half-decent outfit, a *buba* and wrapper made from turquoise guinea brocade. I was even wearing a head tie. Grace had expertly twisted the modest strip of material into what she called the British Airways style, after the navy folded hats their stewardesses used to wear.

"You French!" he shouted. "You makin' trouble for this Nigeria-o."

Nigeria was having a diplomatic incident with nearby Cameroon over the border territory of the Bakassi Peninsula. It was a dispute that had simmered for years and was not to be resolved for another decade. The French government had got involved. This seemed to be the reason the army were on the Badagry Expressway to monitor traffic coming from the border with the Benin Republic.

"I'm not French," I said. "I have no idea what you're talking about."

He looked nonplussed, as if he didn't believe a word I was saying.

"She is not French," Grace had jumped out of the car. She was now standing waving her finger and shouting at him.

"She is not French," Margaret, who had joined her, bellowed.

"Now leave her alone."

"You say you are not French. But you are coming from that side. Where is your passport?"

I didn't have my passport.

"Listen-o. This woman is not a French. She stays with us. She is from UK."

Grace had turned to face the soldier and was standing in the road shouting, hands on her hips. The elaborate gauze head-tie she'd carefully crafted this morning as she prepared for an outing to the city jiggled threateningly on her head as she shook it at him. He turned his rifle towards her. And then she began to tear a strip off him, telling him that here was a foreigner from Britain and he was shaming Nigeria by his behaviour.

He belched again and lurched towards her. For a minute, I thought he was going to push her against the car. He started shouting again, raising his rifle into the air. He was either drunk or unhinged. The idea of having a go at a soldier in possession of a rifle had terrified me so much I was shaking.

And then suddenly it was all over.

"Get back in the car," he snarled.

Grace turned on the heels of her jewelled sandals and proceeded to get into the passenger seat, pulling the door to with an emphatic bang. Margaret had already scuttled into the back of the car. I slid into the driving seat, revved up the engine and a purring Stanley spirited us away.

As we re-entered the fray, I thought about those lines that were drawn when European powers sat in a boardroom in Paris and carved up Africa. The straight line that had been drawn through the Oba's sitting room continued down through lands and homes to the sea. French on one side, British on the other. The eastern border of Nigeria had been fashioned in a similar way; it included a river that wasn't a river, Rio del Rey, which was at the epicentre of the current conflict. As the British Prime Minister, Lord Salisbury, said in 1890:

> We have been engaged in drawing lines upon maps where no White man's foot ever trod; we have been giving away mountains and rivers and lakes to each other, only hindered by the small impediment that we never knew exactly where the mountains and rivers were.

Perhaps that soldier was right to turn on me, the white European, with the blame for Bakassi.

HUMANISING ANTHROPOLOGY

When we got back from Lagos, I scurried to my little hiding place on the roof of the house to mull things over. The encounter with the soldier was a sharp reminder of how saturated everything was with the legacy of colonialism. Me, my project, anthropology, my very presence in this place. I could barely think outside it.

It prompted me to push myself to define more closely what it meant for why I was there and what I was doing. I began to think about an anthropology – one that I had barely yet encountered, but which I felt could and should exist – that was in dialogue with people's versions of themselves, rather than rendering them its object. An anthropology that was dedicated to Anthropos, that which is human. A human*ised* anthropology,. One that did not reduce people to being *just like us*, disregarding difference. One that did not position others at such a distance that they became *them*, the *Other*. An anthropology so deeply infused with what Patricia Hill Collins calls an 'ethic of care' that it could make us more fully aware of our humanity and, through that, more fully human.

I'd come across Patricia Hill Collins' book *Black Feminist Thought* shortly before I left for Nigeria. It wasn't on any of my reading lists. Nor was it to be found in our library. I'd chanced on it in a feminist book shop in Islington. It was radical, refreshing, challenging. Life changing. It gave me a whole new perspective.

I read it as a white woman sitting with the discomfort that

the discipline of anthropology and its canon had stoked in me. She spoke of the possibility of an entirely different approach to knowledge and knowing. She begins the book by dismantling the idea that the path to knowledge begins with separating yourself from what you are studying and striving for objectivity. To be objective, you need to stop yourself from feeling and set aside your values. You need to remove your own being from your research so entirely that you can claim that it is free of your beliefs, your ethics, your principles. To do this, she suggests, would have the consequence of taking you further and further away from being human.

Patricia Hill Collins threw off all the pretence that surrounds the production of knowledge about human beings by other human beings. I'd found the very idea of anthropologists being able to produce objective, value-free, knowledge quite barmy on a human level. How can you live amongst people as intimately as an anthropologist does for such extended periods of time and stop yourself from feeling anything, whether sadness, irritation, affection, or dislike? Surely the way people react to anthropologists is because of who we are as people, as humans? Aren't our questions shaped by our own human experience, otherwise why would we find something novel or curious or interesting? And how was it possible to imagine that the research that anthropologists do isn't ultimately as much about them and the things that they think are worth investigating or reporting as about the people they study?

As I read Patricia Hill Collins' book, I was gripped by her words and their powerful message, affirming the humanity in the process of research, bringing us back to what matters: empathy, compassion, and personal accountability.

I sat for a while up there on the roof letting the memory of those words sink in. That I was in Nigeria at all was an outcome of a story of accumulation, greed, conquest, and corruption that was the British empire. I'd grown up on the fruit of its spoils.

I'd been educated in the Enlightenment fiction that there was Truth to be found through the exercise of reason and empirical investigation. Those whom my education had extolled as the thinkers whose writings would lead us there were without exception white and male. No other form of knowledge was acknowledged, nor was the racism of those thinkers attributed to them.

Studying anthropology had opened the possibility of there being other ways to know and understand the world. But I'd remained with a prickling feeling that the same treatment of beliefs wasn't being administered liberally enough to the ways of the white anthropologists who taught my generation as it was to those of the cultures they studied. *Our* culture never merited as much inspection as *theirs*.

My perch on the roof had come to feel like a liminal zone between worlds. It was the only place where I could be quite alone, detached from the mill of everyday life around me. I'd sit there at dusk on the unfinished concrete steps drawing on a cigarette, with a warm beer from Romeo's Cool Spot by my side, ruminating. The scene drew an unseemly contrast with the flowery-dressed Mrs Mainstream. It was what I came to think of as the *real me*.

As the night descended and the mosquitoes settled in for a feast, I got up, turned off the rumination switch and headed back down the steps to 'the field'. Patricia Hill Collins might have prompted me to question the very idea of objectivity, but I still had habits I'd cultivated to do the work of the proper anthropologist with that I needed to shake off.

I can't honestly remember what triggered it, but within minutes I had been transformed into a fury. I'd come downstairs, headed towards my room, and then something happened that made me lose my rag. I am someone who hardly ever loses their temper. I can probably count on the fingers of one hand the number of times I've shouted at people. I just don't do shouty. I'm not exactly placid, but I'm someone who is more likely to burst into tears than into rage.

Whatever it was, I remember standing there in the hallway and screaming at the top of my voice.

"I've had it!"

It was like the way people described being possessed by a spirit. My anger had transformed me into a totally different character. Like a volcano, spewing a glowering stream of molten lava.

I raged on, "I'm sick of it. Sick. Of. It."

Baba Tinu stood there timidly. He stared at me, wild-eyed. His jaw dropped and stayed there. Frozen.

The children came running. They'd heard the *oyinbo* shouting. It was a new, unusual sound. Not that the sound of arguing was unfamiliar in the mud plaster house, its rooms separated by thin walls, its ceilings made of matting that would catch the faeces of the gekkos who roamed in the rafters. Iya Tinu could be heard of an evening taking her wastrel of a husband to task, tearing a strip out of him, roaring his uselessness, his drunkenness, his folly. Ayomide, Tade and Bolanle might occasionally be chastised by their parents or fall foul of Iya Tinu, who was known for her short temper. Even Baba Tinu, the mildest of characters, was known to have an occasional shouting fit.

It was part of everyday life. Arguments would well up suddenly like a massive wave that took you completely by surprise, loom in front of you and then crash into you, pushing you back with their force.

But in the midst of all this loss of temper, no-one had ever seen me in anything but a state of mild acceptance.

And there I was, losing it.

Within minutes we were all laughing. I got the giggles, and stood there breathless and gasping, my eyes watering with the mirth of it all. I'd gone and lost my temper, not what would be ever expected of the good anthropologist, and certainly not of the polite English Mrs Mainstream.

Somehow, that day, I became human, as fallible in my humanity as a Yoruba deity.

THE PARTICIPATORY TURN

I'd no sooner settled into the rhythm of my research than I started wrestling with a very un-anthropological desire. I wanted to do something for the people whose time I was taking with my questions. Rather than just stockpile the things they told me and put them in my thesis for my own good, I wanted to give something back.

It was a classic folly, one that was almost bound to come my way as a white person. I'd been schooled by media reports, mailshots and billboard ads that represented Africa as a place in need. For all that I could muster a harsh critique of the political economy of the aid industry, somehow there still lurked in my subconscious the idea that where there was poverty and suffering, there should be Development. And through Western eyes, I saw that need all around me.

I chewed all this over with Margaret. We fell to discussing what was being done by development juggernauts like the World Bank. But I still had a place in my heart at that time in my life for well-intentioned efforts to help. Even if I also recognised that when they involved white people like myself, they were tarnished with the brushings of white privilege and the self-aggrandising aspirations of white saviourism. I also still had a sense of guilt. Burdening people with my questions without any benefit to them. Imposing my presence. Extracting their stories, their knowledge. All of this weighed heavily on me.

"Just focus on your studies," Margaret counselled.

I could see her point. But participatory methods were surely a way to democratise my research, give those who are so often the subjects of other people's questions the opportunity to ask their own questions, reveal their own realities, enable them to empower themselves. What was not to love about my ethnographic research taking a participatory turn? I'd spent some years working as a trainer in a new approach to research that involved getting people to draw pictures and use symbols rather than wait for the researcher to hit on the right question to ask. It was called Participatory Rural Appraisal, or PRA.

Anthropologists had no time for PRA. They mocked it as pseudo-science. Quick and dirty. Never mind that many participatory methods were borrowed from a most respectable anthropological methods primer, Pelto and Pelto's 1978 book *Anthropological Research: The Structure of Inquiry.* I'd met the guru of PRA, got hooked, became an enthusiast, and travelled the world teaching people how to get people in local communities drawing pictures that represented the significant things in their worlds and using these to come up with solutions to the problems they faced. It became my guilty secret.

It was as close as I ever got to understanding what drove missionary zeal.

I'd more or less given all of that up before I started my fieldwork, convinced that what I was about to do was Proper Anthropology. The Real Thing was, however, not quite all it was cracked up to be. All that participating and observing and scribbling away in my fieldnotes. It was such an individualistic way to do research. The anthropologist became the judge of what was worth knowing, taking away their notebooks to construct an authoritative version of a People or a Culture. Iya Dayo had introduced the topic of how women make their money. Now it was time to turn my research over to women who were the ones making the money and invite them to pose their own questions.

That's how I found myself sitting on a bench under a raffia shelter in a yard full of fetid vats of fermenting *fufu* with a piece of bamboo and a pile of stones, trying to interest a group of women in a method called Matrix Ranking. The basic idea was that rather than ask people questions, getting them to do drawings or borrow simple templates from maths like Venn diagrams, bar charts and pie chart gave insights into their categories and concepts that would be harder to gain through conversation alone.

I'd chosen a method that involved taking similar things and working out criteria by which to rate them against each other, then giving each of them a score against those criteria. I hadn't surfaced the underlying assumptions I was making, which I would soon find myself stumbling over awkwardly.

I'd cleared a little patch of mud between the benches, lightly dusting it with fine earth to create a makeshift drawing board. The women were looking at me curiously. It was boiling hot. A baby was fretting. The women were passing him between them, jiggling him on their knees, trying to get him to smile. He wasn't going to be cajoled. Someone took him off to seek cool in the darkened bowels of the mud-plaster house. An older woman came by with a basket of kola nuts and stopped for a rest on the end of one of the benches. She picked through the basket, throwing out nuts that had begun to turn and holding out a handful to the woman sitting next to me.

Kola was the queen of trades. It was expensive to get into and dominated by older women for this reason; it was rare to begin with it, it was the kind of trade you worked up to, amassing the capital you'd need for your supply. It ran in families. The amount of capital needed to purchase enough supply to go to market was prohibitive. Suppliers were choosy extending credit only through close contacts. Those who gained the opportunity to sell preserved their market carefully in low, deep baskets. They'd crouch on their heels picking over the kola, swift fingers flicking out any trace of mildew. In the market, they sat close and fierce together. Kola traders rarely wore the cheap local cloth that was all that the sellers who traded in leafy green vegetables could afford. This one was wearing coral-coloured guinea brocade, with the kind of head tie that would be more commonly seen in church, a gaudy, flouncy confection. She lingered, clearly intrigued by the incongruous presence of the white woman.

I sat poised with my bamboo stick in hand, waiting for a lull in the conversation so that I could begin. I cleared my throat. I started with the *I am here in Nigeria* line, explaining how I was studying at the university and doing a project on women's work. I then explained that I was going to ask them about the different job options women in Ilemi had by drawing a box with smaller boxes into it on the ground. I'd then ask them, I said, to choose what to put into the boxes.

They looked amused. *At least I have their attention,* I thought. I proceeded to draw a matrix with the stick in the red earth.

"What kinds of things did you think about when you were considering what kind of job you'd like to have?" I asked, smiling with encouragement.

Iya Dayo duly translated my words.

There was silence.

They broke into an animated chat. I couldn't grasp a single word of it.

"What are they saying, Iya Dayo?".

"They're saying what are you asking," she said. "They're saying these are the trades we learnt when we were young, that one needs capital, that one can be done with very little capital,

105

that one always has a problem with creditors, that one is very backbreaking as the baskets are so heavy. That's what they're talking about."

I tried to get them interested in filling in the matrix. I'd brought some index cards with me to draw pictures on. I led off on the question of starting capital, a defining feature in women's ability to trade. I drew a large Naira symbol. I put the card on the matrix. I went on drawing on the cards, building up a column of cards representing the different criteria that Iya Dayo had listed.

"What else is important?" She put the question to them.

"Family." She translated as they spoke. "They say family, what your mother and your sisters and your father's sisters and mother do. You follow them when you're small and little by little you learn those kinds of work from them."

I drew some stick figures on an index card.

"What else?"

"The husband. If he's the kind that wants you to stay close to the house, or the kind who won't keep on asking you where you are going."

I drew another stick figure. This was tough going.

"What else?"

"Some kinds of work are very hard. Gathering firewood for example. You can end up with thorns in your body and it's heavy to carry. Others are not so hard. Like selling cloth. It's clean work, you don't get dirty. But to make money you need to be willing to travel to buy the cloth and you need money for that, as well as having the problem of people buying on credit and then not paying, so it's not always easy."

Slowly, the column of criteria took shape. I could sense the women were getting bored.

"OK, now let's think some more about the kinds of work women do. Can you ask them if they can list some other kinds of work?"

The women dutifully listed. Kola. Pepper. Vegetable. Cloth. Making *fufu*. Extracting palm oil.

I drew symbols for each on index cards and placed them in a row at the top of the matrix. The next step was to go through the criteria one by one and give each a score out of ten. I'd brought a bag of dried black-eye beans for the purpose.

I grabbed a handful of beans and gave a quick demonstration. It was a bit like *ayo olopon*, that game that men play in the shade in the hot sun of the afternoon, scooping up and distributing beans across a carved board with a sequence of little hollows. I narrated my scores as I distributed the beans.

The women became animated, "no, not so!" and "that's it!".

I cleared off the beans and dipped again into the bag, opening my hand as I offered them the beans to come and do the scoring.

It must have been more than an hour later that we exhausted the last thing that could be said about the choices of jobs that many Ilemi women have. And what had we learnt? Life is hard. The economic situation, defaulting on credit, suspicious husbands, childcare responsibilities, difficulties with suppliers, customers running out of cash. As for choice, for these women, there was no such thing as being able to just choose one kind of work over another.

One explained that since she was a small girl, she'd worked with the pepper sellers in her family. Her mother had taught her how to trade. As a young girl, she'd minded her mother's stall in the mid-afternoon sun when there are hardly any customers to be had. Now she was in her 60s and everyone knew her as Iya Alata, mother of pepper. Pepper was not only her life's work. It was also her identity. How could she have thought of doing anything else? How would she have learnt? Who would she be now without pepper?

And was the first and last time I inflicted participatory methods on the women we spent our days amongst. I'd like to hope that Iya Dayo was grateful for the small mercy of not having to go through all of that again.

CAREER
OPPORTUNITIES

The matrix ranking episode may not have yielded its promised participatory effects. But it got me asking the questions I'd had about women's work in Ado of myself. How, I wondered, had *I* come to be doing what I was doing right now? What made me choose to be an anthropologist? Was it a deliberate, conscious, rationally calculated, risk assessed, cost/benefit analysed choice? Was it something that came from an emotional connection with the work itself? Or was it an identification with what it meant to be known as someone who is an Anthropologist, like Iya Onibata is known to work with trading shoes or Iya Elefo with vegetable leaves?

I'd found out about anthropology on an acupuncturist's couch, stuck full of needles, as I'd narrated the dead end I'd come to in my life.

"What is it that you like to do?" said the acupuncturist, her tone calm and helpful.

"Working with people," I said.

"What kind of work can you see yourself doing?" she asked.

"I wanted to be a doctor," I told her. "Then I went to a medical school for an interview. I was introduced to a group of medical students. They were all men. They joked about cadavers and pickled organs in jars."

I could see myself in the strange-smelling building that they'd taken me to, with its long, dark wood tables where dissections were performed and the tall shelves full of glass jars of body parts in formaldehyde.

"Suddenly I felt revulsed. It was the whole idea that I could end up like them. That becoming a doctor might mean being trained not to see people, just bodies. And then the idea of what would happen if I couldn't save people and they died. That I'd be responsible for them living or dying."

"How did that make you feel?" she asked.

"It felt really heavy. I couldn't imagine having that much responsibility. I didn't stop and think much about it. I just knew that I couldn't go through with it."

How I got to anthropology from there, I couldn't quite remember. But we'd talked about people, and how I was intrigued by them. Of how I'd tried studying psychology and how it felt like the very opposite of how or what I'd want to know about people. Of how I loved reading fiction because it gave me a window into other people's worlds. Of how intrigued I'd been when I'd travelled to other countries and seen how differently people relate to the world.

"Social anthropology," she announced. "Check it out. I've got a feeling that it would be perfect for you."

And it was. Perfect.

I'd embarked on a degree, taking a course that could lead to a career. But would it be a career in anthropology? Mulling it over as I listened to women describing their working lives, some of them narrating the moment they'd struck upon the line of trade they'd go on to pursue, others the long and arduous struggles they'd had to find a way to make a living before they'd settled into a particular form of livelihood, I realised I'd never really stopped and thought about what it meant to have a career. I wasn't sure I was choosing one now, even if I guess the point of carrying on studying was to figure out what I wanted to do with my life.

There was nothing so clear as a *choice* to it.

Career. I turned the word over in my mind some more. Built into the idea of 'having a career' is progress towards an end-state of success. This can be achieved step by step by making *career choices*. *Career prospects* and *career highlights* carry this sense of motion and a defined sense of accomplishment. The *career advice* that's given at school and when people are out of a job invites us to think of what we might do with our working lives. "What do you want to do when you grow up?" was a question I was asked a lot as a child, growing up in an almost exclusively white neighbourhood on the aspiring edges of an otherwise impoverished north-eastern English city. When I was grown up, it had changed to, "what do you *do*?" where *to do* was to have a job, a profession, a career.

For quite some while I didn't *do*. I worked and received a wage. I spent long hours in service jobs, balancing plates, clearing tables, cleaning up after people. I got my jobs because I was young and presentable enough to be a waitress. I got tips because I was obliging, efficient and friendly. I mastered the art of carrying six cups on one arm, an achievement unmatched by anything I subsequently did as an academic. While I acquired professional skills, I didn't think of what I did as a profession as such. I recognised that some of my colleagues specialised in this line of work. I just did it because it was the only job I could get. It wasn't a career. It was just work.

Many of my jobs involved casual employment in catering, an industry so precarious I could bedismissed at any time. And I was sacked from one of those restaurants, once, for organising the kitchen workers to demand the right to take a holiday. The restaurant was right in the very heart of London's tourist centre. It employed glamorous looking waiting and bar staff. I dolled myself up, black eyeliner, short skirt and artfully arranged hair. I would glide between the glitz of the restaurant area, all shiny mirrors and marble and tasteful tablecloths, and the grime of the hot, crowded kitchen.

There was a clear racial division of labour. All the waiting staff were white. All the kitchen staff were not. But we had one thing in common. We were all denied the opportunity to take leave. We were all on casual contracts. The restaurant paid us a pittance. The white staff earned a decent living from tips. But there was no mechanism to redistribute these gains to the mostly Black kitchen staff, who subsisted on long shifts for achingly low wages. Being disposable meant that if anyone stepped out of line, they would find ourselves out of a job. And that's what I did. Because I could.

To be honest, I hadn't really had a clue what I'd do with my life once I'd abandoned the safe career choice that "I'd like to be a doctor" represented for all those years. Part of the trouble I had explaining to people why I was doing what I was doing - beyond the obvious pursuit of a degree - was that I'd never really had much of a story about what I wanted to do with my life.

If the ever-curious anthropologist that asked those women all those questions about their working lives had turned their attention to me, they'd have found me struck by the extent to which serendipity played a defining role in making me who I am. A chance conversation with an acupuncturist. A visit to a friend, studying in a college I'd never heard of before. A journey on a *danfo* to a place I wouldn't reach for many months that deposited me en route at the stall of the person who was to become my closest friend, and who so generously took me in and offered me a home. There wasn't much in any of this that was akin to a *career choice*. I wasn't even sure that I wanted to be an anthropologist when I embarked on the path that was to take me to Nigeria.

One of the things that happens a lot to anthropologists is that we pause like this, to inspect words and concepts that we might up to that point have taken for granted. It can happen in the moment when we compare our concepts with those of another people, feeling the slight strangeness of something that was before so familiar it didn't invite question. It can be when a term *seems* to mean the same as it does in the context in which you'd originally come to know it, but the meaning turns out to be something quite different.

In that jolt of difference comes an insight into what the American philosopher Nelson Goodman called *ways of worldmaking.*

"A description is right and a statement is true," Goodman argued, *"for a world it fits".*

I remember reading that and having one of those moments when the world as you know it suddenly becomes something strange and extraordinary, and nothing looks the same again. Like a psychedelic experience. But anthropologists don't generally need to take drugs for this to happen. They just need to remain open, turn on and tune in.

If people's understandings of the world are right for the world they fit, I reflected, the task of the anthropologist becomes that of an interpreter who moves between worlds, immersing themselves in them to listen to those statements and understand the worlds in which they fit, and then helping build bridges between them.

BRIDGE BUILDER

I liked the idea of the anthropologist as builder of bridges between worlds. It felt as if it was constructive. Purposeful. Not just the *bricoleur*, putting together fragments and making them do the work at hand – a concept I'd learnt from reading French anthropologist Claude Lévi-Strauss in my second-year undergraduate class. The metaphor of bridge-builder connoted doing something actively directed at building understanding.

But whose understanding was served by this bridge building?

Anthropology was born in the era of empire; it is, more than any other discipline, a colonial science. Anthropologists put their services at the disposal of empires past. They were sent to gather intelligence and act as interlocutors with the subjects of colonial rule, relaying information to colonial authorities. Not for nothing did Talal Asad write of anthropology as being the *handmaiden of colonialism*.

As the era of colonial rule receded, anthropologists began to reflect critically on what it meant to collude with colonialism. It was a complicated relationship. There was not only the obvious kind of collusion, where anthropologists would use their skills to gather information on matters of interest to the authorities. This could be, for example, how people might react if certain policies were to be introduced. Anthropologists have continued to provide these kinds of services to international development agencies and market research companies. They could potentially be labelled as colluding with neo-colonialism or neo-liberalism for their sins.

There was also a more subtle kind of collusion. The very topics that anthropologists worked on and the very ways in which they produced knowledge were in themselves of service to the colonial powers. Those old-style ethnographies that I'd seen as a fallback option when I lost my topic were accounts of many different facets of life in places where colonisers faced the puzzle of how best to negotiate with and manage those under their dominion. Colonial officials could go to study at a place like SOAS and read the works of anthropologists, learning from them about the countries for which they were to form or were already part of the colonial administration. Anthropologists produced accounts of political organisation, the way political discourse was used in meetings, modes of exchange and how the economy was organised, conflict and cooperation. All this information was, of course, of great use to those who sought quiescence as they expanded empire.

Anthropology willingly served other masters. Victorian-era American anthropologist Lewis Henry Morgan and his followers categorised and indexed peoples, placing them on an evolutionary scale. It doesn't take a huge leap of imagination to work out where this ended up, especially at a time when belief in eugenics was rife. Sir James Fraser's *Golden Bough* represented a different kind of anthropology. Filled with all manner of rites and rituals, magic and taboos, from around the world, it came to stand for a kind of anthropology that filled museums with unusual artefacts, an exhibit of exotica. The British Museum continues this tradition, the keynotes of their Africa section being collections of feathered carved masks; a place where visitors can feed representations of Africa as primitive, full of strange rituals. Rather like the book about the masquerade that brought me to Nigeria in the first place.

Robert Chambers memorably described anthropologists' writings as *long and lost*. It takes ages to produce, ages to read and as a result, he suggested, it gets lost and loses its usefulness. Written not just in English, but in a kind of English that is as abstruse as it is dry, peppered with jargon, most ethnographies take a certain amount of toil to plough through. I'd come to recognise that to get to the story, I needed to skip to the middle of the article or the book and read that bit first, then go back and see what the author was trying to do with it. It wasn't the most conventional approach to reading a book. But it made wading through turgid, laboured preambles more digestible. Not for nothing is there an initiative, spearheaded by American anthropologist Bob Borofsky, to promote a 'popular anthropology' that can be read by and reach a wider audience and that's relevant to the challenges of the contemporary world.

I mulled over all of this as I thought about what I was going to write. I reflected on what it might mean to want to become an anthropologist: to make doing anthropology my *career*. There was precious little else offered to the budding anthropologist than the prospect of becoming one of the professors who taught us. These people seemed to have comfortable enough lives. I'd been to the houses of a few of them. They were without exception large, with expansive libraries, full of ornaments brought back from the countries in which they'd done their fieldwork and ethnic chic. It was not a bad life. And then there were those legendary long academic holidays where all, I imagined, the anthropologist had to do – if they hadn't departed for The Field - was to brush off the dust from their fieldnotes and knock out another article for the *Journal of the Royal Anthropological Institute* or some similarly august publication.

I'd grown up with the need for a sense of purpose. I wasn't quite able to imagine how I'd find my purpose contributing to the state of ethnographic knowledge about Nigeria. So far, I'd left a trail of failure behind me. I'd ditched my original project, without having anything to replace it. I'd cut short my time at the school. I'd had a dismal attempt at participatory research, quickly abandoning it with a shudder at how it might have made people feel. I'd started a promising line of enquiry into the impact of economic change on people's lives, but it led nowhere. That structural adjustment caused misery was not a novel finding. Nor did I have means to do anything about it.

I wasn't exactly treading water. I spent every day dutifully and diligently interviewing people, participant observing where I could. Every night, I could be found writing my fieldnotes by the light of my paraffin lamp. But I still didn't have a clue why I was doing all this, or how it would come together in the end. What was it all for? What was my thesis going to be about?

I reflected on how deeply the kind of benevolent paternalism that saturates international development had permeated my own being. I'd been carrying around with me a deep sense of guilt about what I was doing. I felt bad about taking up people's time with my questions. I had wrestled with angst about having given up on a project that had at least had some kind of benefit to people in mind, even if was one that they themselves might not have chosen or recognised as such.

Why did I think I could do anything to 'help'? Where did this desire to help come from and why, if I had that desire, had I come to Africa to visit it on people there? Why wasn't I working for the British National Health Service or doing something else useful, if that was what was driving me? Was anthropology in any way useful? Or was it simply a colonial residue that was kept alive by people like me being attracted to what it offered us – adventures in foreign places, conversations across cultures, the almost smug feeling that we were somehow floating above life, making sense of it all?

What if, I wondered, what if an anthropologist did was to enable people who had very different ways of worldmaking to understand each other, rather than grasping onto the most obscure bits of different cultures and describing them in ways that make them sound truly strange, then analysing all this in language so complex and jargon-ridden that they become even stranger? What if in explaining about how things work in another culture and drawing explicit parallels and contrasts with their own, the anthropologist could make the familiar curious as well as help confront racist prejudices about those from other countries?

Rather than being some omnipresent, all-knowing Expert, what if the anthropologist were to pride themselves in their skills in finding out rather than in their knowledge? And what if that anthropological skill were put not only to valuing the integrity of other ways of knowing and being, but also to creating greater human understanding?

Asking these questions shifted something inside me. There was something there that I hadn't quite got to grips with yet. But I felt lighter, somehow. I was starting to see the point of what I was doing.

RAIN, RAIN GO AWAY

The rainstorm had dragged on for four days. It was unrelenting. The hammering of drops on the corrugated iron roof kept me awake at night. It poured in through the grille on my window and dripped from the rafters. The passageway that ran through the middle of our house was pocked with muddy puddles from leaks in the roof. No work could be done when it rained like this. Iya Dayo stayed at home. I'd peer out of the doorway and see the occasional figure running from porch to porch. But the town came more or less to a halt. It could go on like this for days.

Nigerian rain is of a completely different quality to the damp, chilly misery of English drizzle. One of the pleasures of living in the tropics is the relief when the heat breaks and the skies open and bathe the earth in a glorious deluge. The dense, cloying air before the downpour begins can be overwhelming. Temperature and tensions rise, tempers fray. Then suddenly it breaks. The smell of sun-baked earth yielding to the first drops of rain is one of my favourite aromas, a sweet freshness mingled with a warm, delicious earthiness.

Years later, the very thought of that smell brings back a scene of standing by our back door, holding it ajar and gazing enchanted at the sight of sheets of water bouncing off the deep red earth. And then going out and dancing around in it with gleeful shouts, revelling in its wet warmth. The sight of the *oyinbo* skipping around in the rain made the children of the compound squeal with mirth. I'd shake the rain off my hair like a dog, and they'd laugh even more.

After four days of being stuck inside I was getting really bored. I'd written up my fieldnotes from the last couple of days. I'd had a stab at analysing the round of interviews Baba Tinu had done for me with men of his age, morose tales of having been taken for a ride by women who they'd tried and failed to please. There was something about masculinity in the confessional he created for them in those interviews, framed by their knowledge of his own experience, that made for a very different story to the ones I was hearing from women. It was an intriguing counterpoint to the complaints about men not being the husbands that they were supposed to be.

I was latching onto something fascinating. The very idea of *husband* was so full of expectation and so ripe for disappointment. But I couldn't get much further without more conversation with Baba Tinu. And as far as I could make out, he'd disappeared to sit and drink *ogogoro* with his mates while the rain provided him with cover.

I felt bad saying I was bored. But it was the truth. I'd read all the books I'd brought with me. I had notebooks full of impressions, quotes, stories, interviews, the occasional diagram and every now and again a little list of things that seemed worth coming back to at some point. They were a record for later. I was still trying to find the storyline for my project. I re-read them regularly. I tried doing the same again, combing through the pages for inspiration. I didn't find any answers in those densely written, numbered pages. It was all reasonably fresh in my mind. If I was honest, it depressed me. I still didn't really have any clue about how it was all going to come together.

Anthropologists are not supposed to get bored. In my mind's eye, the anthropologist is forever watching, notebook in hand, intrigued by what they see. They aren't supposed to disagree with people. They aren't supposed to find people dull or objectionable. And they aren't supposed to start fantasising about dipping a piece of freshly baked Lebanese flatbread into a bowl of hummus with a thin dusting of vermillion-red paprika and a golden well overflowing with spicy, fragrant olive oil...

My mouth began to water. I decided to get Stanley and go to Ibadan for a couple of days. I'd at least be able to go to the archives and do some more nosing around in colonial record books. I was a bit of a dilettante when it came to dredging the records. I had none of the patient rigour of the historian. I'd gather up armfuls of reports and flip through them, looking for any nuggets that looked promising. I wasn't entirely sure what I was looking for. I think I'd somehow got the idea that riffling through archives was like browsing in a flea market, chancing on finds. I got distracted easily. The last time I was there, I'd discovered a catalogue of back issues of the main Nigerian newspapers, including – to my delight – *Lagos Weekend*. I'd taken to calling up volumes from the 1970s to accompany the rather dull search through the administrative records of the colonial authorities. The ribald humour and outrageous stories in those pages could keep me amused for weeks.

I stuffed some flowery dresses into a plastic bag, ripped a hole in a bin liner and tugged it over my head to protect my clothes, topping it off with a carrier bag that I fashioned into a hairnet to protect myself from spending the next few hours in a soaking mess.

I tripped down the steps to tell Grace that I was going to the university for a few days. I knew what she would say. And she did.

"Ann, please. Driving in this rain. Why not wait until it stops?

"But that's the point," I said, "it's not stopping".

The first part of the journey was the easiest. The route then took me onto a major road with fast-moving traffic. It was raining so hard that I had to keep flicking on the wipers every few minutes. I'd picked up a lot of Nigerian driving habits and this was one of them: not keeping the wipers on all the time, just using them to clear the windscreen when it was so crowded with rivulets of water it was hard to see anything. I still have it. I've rationalised it as something about the sound of windscreen wipers that irritates me.

The rain was dripping inside the car as well, gathering in a cold pool under my feet. I hadn't managed to protect the lower half of my body, so I was now sitting in the sticky dampness of Stanley's burgundy velveteen drivers' seat. Every so often, the car in front would brake suddenly and I'd have flashbacks of careering in slow motion and then the merciless crunching sound as Stanley's carapace crumpled. I'd forgotten about the hummus by then.

Grace was right. Grace was always right.

And then the rain abated. The sky lifted and the traffic thinned out. Soon Stanley and I were sailing again. A bright ray of sunlight threw a rainbow across the sky. I slowed as we rolled through one of the many little towns along the route. Women sat under tarpaulins, laughing. Men sat huddled together in rows on wooden benches under porches. Children were playing, jumping off steps into puddles, giggling.

I suddenly had a feeling wash over me. It brought me out in goosebumps. I later came to know it as *sonder*: the knowledge that all around me there are people living their own lives, with their own pasts and futures and that being just one tiny part of what it means to be human. My anthropologist's curiosity might feel as if it was boundless. But there were always going to be people I'd never met, stories I'd never get to hear, experiences I'd never be able to share. Nor could I ever really capture or explain all that makes up the complexity of the human condition in this or any other place, even if I were to spend the rest of my life studying it.

With that came a sense of deep relief. Something settled inside me that had been restlessly searching since I arrived in Nigeria, needling me for a sense of purpose or a set of propositions that could make up my thesis. Suddenly, it didn't seem so intimidating any more. It felt as if I just needed to be open to what came along. Just as I'd found a fieldsite, I would find my thesis. It would come.

CRI DE COEUR

Stanley came back from Ibadan with the car equivalent of a sore throat. His carburettor was all choked up again and he was rasping. I'd taken him straight to the yard of my mechanic Remi, where he stood hunched over an engine covered in motor oil with a clutch of apprentices fidgeting around him. Remi had pulled off his best trick, coaxing Stanley's carburettor into a soft purr with a piece of finely folded cigarette paper. It worked like magic every time.

I was sitting at my desk later that day, writing up the day's fieldnotes, when I'd heard the distinctive tap-tap of knuckles on my door. Remi had a habit of calling by in the evening for a chat. A stocky man in his late 30s, with a close shaven head, he was rarely seen out of his mechanic's overalls. He'd sit by my table, chain smoking, I'd sit on the end of my bed, and he'd launch into long and often deeply philosophical monologues.

"*C'est la coeur de la voiture,*" Remi said, gesticulating extravagantly with his cigarette. I watched as its smouldering end fell onto the mat and began to sizzle. Surreptitiously, I ventured the tip of my shoe to stub it out, wincing at the burn mark.

"*Quoi?*" I asked, not yet following what he'd come to impart to me.

Today's talk was about the nature of cars and their essential resemblance to human beings. I'd come to know more about

Stanley's innards through these conversations than the hours spent peering into his bonnet whilst Remi or his boys worked on him. It was a habit I was instructed by Grace and Margaret not to continue. For all that he'd pay me social visits, in their view he was not to be trusted.

Remi itemised each part of the car, then drew out the analogy piece by piece.

We'd got to the engine.

The engine, Remi said, was like a human heart. It could get clogged up with dirt and build up residues of spent oil that were like plaques that stopped the blood circulating smoothly through the veins and arteries of the body. He would listen to the sound of the engine, like a doctor listened to a person's heart with their stethoscope, and he could pinpoint exactly what the problem was.

Remi was a master of improvisation. He'd spun me some far-fetched tales about what Stanley needed, including one major piece of surgery that I decided was elective and gently refused. I generously interpreted this as a way he could keep the flow of conversation going and not just my regular contributions to his pay packet. His repair works did not last long, though. I found myself a regular at his garage. My French improved with leaps and bounds. Opening my mouth in Paris some years later as I ordered some bread, a guttural West African French emerged that made the shop assistants giggle. I spoke as I'd learnt it, in the mechanic's yard.

The town was full of imported vehicles of various provenance. Most were older models that had reached the end of their natural lives in Europe and then been shipped in large containers to Lagos for the Nigerian market. There were dozens of Stanley's kindred, Peugeot 504 saloons or estates, in various states of disrepair. Lots of older Japanese models, cheap and cheerful. Occasionally, there was a newer little Nissan or Honda. And always there were the showiest Mercedes-Benz, all shimmering gold and silver and plush interiors. Kings of the road. There was a brisk trade in car parts that extended into one of the more lucrative lines plied by cross-border smuggling networks.

Remi's diagnosis of Stanley's condition was a simple one. This was a car built for France, not for Nigeria. Stanley's very Frenchness was the basic issue; the car, he said, was going to need to adapt to this Nigeria. But for that to be possible, genuine French parts were needed. Not the ones made in the East. *The East* was synonymous with all things fake. It referred to the places where things are fabricated to pass off as genuine. East could mean eastern Nigeria or East Asia: both were seen by people in the town as sources of fake parts, fake medicine, and all manner of other fake stuff that you couldn't count on for your life.

For all his eloquent musings on the nature of French colonialism, France was for Remi the source of the solid, the trustworthy and the reliable. And, of course, all that reassurance came at a price.

With his two brothers, Remi had come to Ilemi in search of his fortune. Growing up close to the Nigerian border, he was fluent in both the local languages, Yoruba and Egun. Not speaking English wasn't of any matter. He and his brother had crossed the border one night, slipping across the bushland through which the white men's line had been drawn, and over into Nigeria. They'd known Beninois living in Ilemi, who were in with the smugglers who moved dozens of jerry cans of fuel across the border at night. The main arteries of the town were lined with small-scale workshops with gaggles of young lads apprenticed to the craft of keeping cars going well beyond the lives they would have led in their original habitat. For a small town, Ilemi had more mechanics, brake and bodywork specialists than I'd ever come across. Remi and his brothers quickly saw that there was a lot of business working on vehicles, and soon they'd been able to set up their own garage.

Over the years, Ilemi had absorbed many travellers. Migrants and refugees had been drawn to Ilemi in times when the very heart of the town had swelled as it accommodated wave after wave of strangers, displaced by war, escaping the terrors of slavery, finding their way to the town through narrow bush paths and riverine routes. Sub-ethnic groups built their own spaces, families their own compounds that housed further incomers. The town was a patchwork of carefully observed social divisions, the Awori indigenes on one side, the Egbado sub-groups on the other, with areas named after the towns from which they had migrated over the course of the previous hundred years. It was only right that my little room on the edge of the market was in a quarter housing some of the most recent.

Remi's sense of belonging, like many of those who came to the town from other places, was provisional. Home was somewhere else. Even those who'd come with parents or relatives as small children, migrants from distant places that they barely knew as home, did not feel as if Ilemi was where they would remain. It was just a temporary resting place, somewhere to make money, have children and go about acquiring the things in life that matter, not where they imagined becoming old. Strangers were known by a collective noun, *alejo*. I fitted rather awkwardly into the category as the only white person in town. We marked our transience, found our comforts, built what we needed for the time that we'd bide before we returned home.

Being Beninois in Ilemi was like being German or French in the UK: from somewhere known, nearby, but utterly foreign all the same. I'd grown up with a sense of never really fitting in. I was white. I sounded British. But my upbringing had left subtle, almost imperceptible, cultural inflections. These made me seek different comforts and form different judgements. I'd grown up with another mother tongue, a secret language that my mother and I would whisper in when we were out. It gave me a different set of cultural referents. I'd sometimes be caught off balance by white English people - generally those who came from the middle or upper classes - saying something that it turned out later they evidently didn't feel or believe. "I don't mind," was one of those phrases that you had to be very watchful of; it usually meant the opposite. "Whatever you like," was another.

Remi and his garage mates kept themselves to themselves. I had a sense that his regular visits to my room to chat to me about poetry, cars and politics was not just for the novelty of befriending a foreigner, or ensuring my continued custom. There was something shared in our *alejo*-ness. Being a stranger played out in all kinds of other ways. Women told me things that they said they had not told another living soul, for fear of what might happen if it were to be indiscreetly whispered or used in other ways. Being from somewhere else became a kind of superpower, permitting me not only to ask all manner of questions, but to hear all manner of answers. They could sense my temporariness, know that I would be here one day and then gone.

There's something in that very transitory nature of anthropological fieldwork that inflects every aspect of the way you live your everyday life when 'in the field'. It's something that doesn't really get talked about. Anthropologists go to stay in far-away places in the expectation that fieldwork is an episode in a longer story that will unfold over the course of their career as repeated visits give rise to papers, books and the warm glow of recognition that comes with a successful academic career. That story always includes arriving and leaving. It doesn't usually involve remaining.

The time-bound nature of fieldwork is one part of it. What the anthropologist does in that time is another. Participant observation involves paying very close attention to what is going on around you. It's a kind of hovering over what's going on, looking down on it as if from a distance. And to do all that observing, you need to keep on paying attention to everyone else who's part of the scene. It's a bit like your story is one you'd be able to tell in the third person, because you've watched the other characters so closely that you can describe them in almost as much detail as you can yourself.

Key to that ability to remain semi-detached is that the anthropologist knows they're able to go home. Their 'field' is almost by definition somewhere they *don't need to* experience things for real. Their involvement in what's going on around them is what the sociologist Mike Drinkwater called 'virtual participation'. I started thinking about how differently I'd be living and relating to people if I'd moved to Ilemi, like Remi, to make a bit of money or even to have a change of scene.

Would I have constructed Mrs Mainstream with such care if I'd been one of those *alejos*? Maybe I would. I might have felt the need to manage appearances and establish a status that would lend me some protection.

I did lots of things in the course of my fieldwork that I would never otherwise do. There were also things I *didn't* do that would have been part of a life I'd have sought to build for myself if I'd moved to Ilemi to stay, rather than for a sojourn as an anthropologist. Would I really have chosen to stay in my little whitewashed room with a tin roof and mud walls that baked in the sun and emitted such heat at night that I'd lie in bed bathed in sweat, fantasising about the town erupting in shouts to announce the return of NEPA? People were right to be curious about this and ask me why I didn't get myself a storey house with a big steel gate. But was this because I knew that I wouldn't be there for long? Was it so that it would feel like more of an adventure, like travelling? Or because I had internalised along with all the other myths about anthropologists that I really ought to be living in a mud hut and this mud plaster house was the closest I could get to it?

Truth is, I much preferred my little room to just about any of the storey houses I'd ever been in. I loved being in the heart of things. I could steal out at night to replenish my stock of cigarettes from hawkers who lined the main street at night, their baskets lit by little flickering paraffin lamps. I could sneak up to the roof and sit there with my beer watching the hubbub in the motorpark, mulling. Most of all, I loved living with a family. Ayomide would come and curl up with a book. Tade and Bisi would stop by and chat about their days. I could try out my efforts to cook comfort foods from home on Baba and Iya Tinu and they'd pull faces and laugh if the food was horrible to them. Bayo and I would talk politics. Grace would drop in while I was writing up my fieldnotes, cook my favourite dishes and watch with pleasure as I ate them, and regale me with stories and sometimes admonishments.

My whiteness was awkwardly plastered all over this, permeating these very questions. Just as I could shrug off the idea of dressing in lace, I had no need to do any status-enhancing or even status-preserving acts. I was an *oyinbo*, simple as that. Whether I lived in a large storey house or in a room with a wooden shutter and iron grille for a window would make little difference to how people responded to me. Whiteness didn't come in shades of grey. As an *oyinbo*, I carried with me whatever people had come to make of white people they'd come across, heard others tell or seen in magazines, newspapers or on the TV. White privilege defined everything; even my being there at all. Strangely or perhaps not so strangely, this is the bit that the white anthropologists whose work I'd read generally tended to leave out of their ethnographies.

NA WA O!

Na wa o! I'd hear it exchanged between friends, hi-fiving. I'd hear it uttered in exasperation and resignation, a shrug of the shoulders word that conveyed a complex bundle of feelings. It would be used to express shock, fear, anger and that sense of things just being as they are. I came to think of it as a cigarette word: I'd smoke a cigarette when I was happy, sad, angry, elated, miserable, amused, bored. *Na wa o!* was as versatile, as satisfying, as expressive.

Na wa o! "Tade, *wa nbe!*" I shouted, summoning the boy who had become classificatory kin, in anthropological parlance: my younger brother. Like Grace, I'd taken to calling him when I needed him to run an errand for me. In seconds, Tade was there. He muttered as he eyed the angry red hand marks trailing down the wall of my room. It looked like dried blood in the dim light of the swiftly gathering dusk. As if someone with bleeding hands had tried to claw their way up the wall, tearing open their hands on the way. I fully expected to find a body, crumpled and inert, on the floor behind my bed.

Na wa o! "Tade," I tried to steady myself, "can you go to the market and get me one of those little bottles of vodka?"

I needed a drink, as well as a cigarette.

I'd parked Stanley minutes earlier. I'd taken Iya Dayo home after we'd spent an entertaining afternoon at one of my favourite herbalists, Dr Akala. Eloquent and garrulous, he could wax lyrical for hours when he got going. He took evident pleasure in the white woman turning up with her notebook and her interpreter to capture his wisdom in close-written script. Even the normally disapproving Iya Dayo had enjoyed today's session, which was all about the harms that could befall people because of jealousy. Our enquiry into the topic of how women made money had taken the direction of exploring the various things that could get in the way.

Malevolent human intention was identified by woman after woman as one of the main obstacles to succeeding in business. Dr Akala regaled us with a litany of cases of what people called 'trouble in the house', a euphemism, we learnt, for jealousy between the women of the house. Co-wives mainly. Dr Akala told us tales of misery. Mystery illnesses, poison being slipped into water jars and causing the victim to balloon or break out in excruciatingly painful hives, phantom pregnancies and repeated miscarriages. Sometimes it was the mother-in-law, he said. Seeing her son love another woman too much. Iya Dayo chimed in, telling one of the apocryphal tales that circulated in the town of the mother-in-law who turned up with a huge fish bone in her bag, then planted it on her plate when the daughter-in-law was out of the room, taking it to complain to her son about how his money was being wasted.

Na wa o! And here I was with trouble of my own to deal with. Tade was back in what felt like seconds, panting from his run to the bottle store. He handed me the bottle of vodka. In a twist the lid was off, and I stood there swigging from the bottle, surveying the scene. As if by magic the light went on in the hallway. I could hear shouts of joy from all around, as if Nigeria had scored in the World Cup. "NEPA! NEPA!". I flicked on the light switch and a white glow filled the room from the bare bulb dangling from the rafter that kept the raffia ceiling in place.

The ceiling. I looked up. One of the raffia mats was displaced. I quickly realised it had been pushed out of the way as the intruder scrambled up the wall. The hand-marks were not blood at all. They were the colour of the dust from the dried red mud that gathered on top of the wall. Against the whitewash, in the half-light, they'd looked like the bloodied trail of fingers clawing the wall as they slid to the ground. Inspecting them more closely in the light, I could see from the pattern of the hand marks that they were from what looked like a couple of people. It looked likely that they'd lowered themselves down and then scrambled, scaling the wall in a hurry to get back over it before I opened the door.

I sat down on my bed, stunned. I'd felt really safe. The house was full of people. Tade, Ayomide and Bisi were all within close reach. We bolted the windows and the doors at night. The house was right next to the motor park and during the day it sat open, with doors at either end ajar. Anyone could find their way in there. But it took some familiarity with the house to find the route through the raffia ceiling into my room. Tade twigged before I could say anything. It must be the cousins. They'd had been given beds in what used to be the storeroom next to my room. They were here for some months lending temporary labour on the farm. I'd hardly seen them. Their room, like mine, was secured with a padlock. It could only be them.

I checked all my hiding places. My money bank wrapper was still hanging on the rail, untouched. I ran my hand down the seam. My fingers lingered on the slight ridges made by the folded bills, barely perceptible to the uninitiated. I'd put bundles of Naira in envelopes and stashed them in my fieldnote books or in the pages of novels. All present and correct. My bulky camera lay on the bottom shelf of the dresser, with a towel slung over it. Nothing seemed to be missing. My first thought was that I'd surprised them by my return. But I hadn't heard the sound of scrambling as the intruders made their way back over the wall. I realised that they'd probably landed in my room expecting treasures or at least a box with money in it and left disappointed.

If I'd been Iya Dayo, I would have crossed myself. Instead, I put the padlock back on the door and headed up to the roof with my vodka bottle and my pack of cigarettes.

The thieves were dealt with swiftly and severely. Brought to their senses about how to behave, taught a lesson. The police being regarded as worse than useless, it had been up to the men of the family to drum some morals into the boys. They came the next day to make their apologies and eyed me sheepishly thereafter.

The episode taught me something that stayed with me throughout the coming months. Even if I didn't much like it that the thieves had been beaten, I'd felt protected, looked after. I continued to feel safe in my little whitewashed room. It also brought a realisation of the extent to which the gruesome tales I'd been told had percolated into my consciousness. Was this what anthropologists called 'going native'?

I was soon to find out.

JUJU

It wasn't until we were clattering along the pot-holed main street in the direction of home that I noticed the black plastic bag sitting on Stanley's dashboard. Iya Dayo and I had just emerged from the fetid darkness of Doctor Yinka's consulting room into the glaring heat of the late afternoon sun, and I was feeling dazed.

Doctor Yinka was one of Ilemi's best-known practitioners of Yoruba traditional medicine. He was famed amongst Ilemi's women for being able to solve the mystery of their infertility. Some claimed that his own libidinous intervention was the source of his results; all concerned were eager to pass this off as the quality of his herbal treatments. The ever-curious anthropologist, I had been angling for a consultation with him for several weeks. Hunched on a hard wooden stool, I'd plied him with dozens of questions, fending off Iya Dayo's disapproving looks. She had a soft spot for Akala and laughed with him when he joked with us. Doctor Yinka was another matter entirely.

Iya Dayo's terse summaries of the streams of Yoruba pouring out of the herbalist's mouth had grated on me all afternoon. We'd had the conversation about translating everything that was said many times, and she had no intention of budging. She'd done all she could to redirect my interest to other, more wholesome, enquiries, taking me that very morning to the compound of the latest of Ilemi's many evangelists, a self-styled prophet who had set up shop near the market. With a discernible sniff of distaste, she had even taken me to the houses of the Muslim *alfas* who lived behind the market. For all that she regarded them with some suspicion, their trade was considerably less dubious than the traditional healers who had so thoroughly captured the white anthropologist's imagination.

Lately, she'd stopped trying to persuade by diversion, and gone instead for a steady drip of criticism. It had started in the car on the way to Dr Yinka's house.

"Why you go see another one of these juju men? They no good-o. They cheat you, they tell you things that will make you go pay them something. They no good. Liars. Thieves."

The tirade of invective halted as she drew her breath before delivering the punchline.

"It is all idolatry." Iya Dayo jabbed accusingly with her finger, and then, as the car hit a pothole, clutched at the dashboard.

The dashboard.

I visualised Iya Dayo's hands gripping an empty expanse of ugly brown plastic; there was nothing on the dashboard when we set out, I was sure.

The car swung from side to side as I negotiated the pocked track of packed red earth that ran between the herbalist's house and ours. The journey was a familiar one, each bump etched into the memories my body was accumulating of my stay. At first, I'd crashed over the craters in the road. That was before I'd learnt to drive Stanley like a Nigerian, hooting my horn with abandon and spinning the steering wheel to swerve around the potholes. I was proud enough of my prowess these days to take my eyes off the road and smile a greeting to those who sat in the shade of their porches enjoying the late afternoon peace before the pace picked up at dusk.

"*Oyinbo!*" the children would shout as I passed, "*Oyinbo!*"

The black plastic bag bumped and rolled along the dashboard. It seemed that it had something round inside it, something that stretched the bag taut around the bottom.

A calabash. With medicine in it.

I banished the thought.

"That bag on the dashboard. Is it yours?" I asked Iya Dayo, trying to sound casual.

"No", Iya Dayo answered. As I glanced quickly at my companion,

I caught Iya Dayo's eyes sweeping over the black plastic package and widening as she traced its shape.

"Are you *sure* it isn't yours, Iya Dayo?" I ventured, with the slightest tremble in my voice. She was silent.

"Well, whose is it?" I wondered aloud. "I don't remember it being in the car when we set off".

"No," said Iya Dayo. "It wasn't there before." She folded her arms and I could see out of the corner of my eye the expression on her face. She exuded exasperation. I'd grown used to her simmering like this for some while and then erupting, upbraiding me for my unwholesome interests much as she would chastise her niece for her waywardness.

We fell into silence. A goat strayed across the road, and I slammed on the brakes. The bag jolted against the windscreen with a hard crack.

It *is* a calabash, I said to myself. *A calabash with juju in it. The kind of juju the herbalist was telling us about. The kind that makes you crash your car, lose your money, your people, your life.*

For a fleeting moment, I wished I'd got religion. Gods and goddesses were things that other people seemed to find some comfort believing in; I couldn't really relate to any of this at all. Sometimes I'd thought of my lack of belief as a failure of the imagination. Most of the time, though, I was quite relieved not to have to carry the burden of all those injunctions. In any case, the way of being religious here was quite different. There was a fluidity in the way people used religion, picking and choosing to suit the circumstance, adapting to other people's predilections and habits – like the newly married women who switched churches, even switched faiths, to fit in with the others in their husband's house.

Religiosity seemed to come along with a kind of pragmatism that I hadn't associated with faith before. Even the most devout would slip off to the herbalist if things were going awry in their lives. They'd steal away with prescriptions for love medicines – *oogun* - to mend broken marriages, to rekindle desire, to dull the impulse to shout or nag, and, if things got really bad, that medicine called *magun* that makes the wandering husband's penis stick to the woman he's sleeping with like superglue.

I smiled as I remembered Grace's attempt to convert me to Catholicism, dragging me along to church with her, and how I'd endured half an hour of the treacherously boring service, sweltering on a hard bench listening to tuneless hymns and long speeches in Latin and Yoruba, before slipping outside for a cigarette.

I could do with a cigarette now.

It had only been a few weeks earlier that I had stood at the edge of my compound watching the blazing orange sun light the sky into an outrageous hot pink. I'd caught the crackling sound of a radio playing an old highlife song. Out from behind the mud plaster houses behind the compound came a little band of children, tumbling along after each other and giggling. "Sisi Anna! Sissi Anna!" the littlest one said, her face breaking into a huge grin as she gazed up at me standing there in my *buba* and wrapper looking into the sky.

Having spied me there, the band of children all came running towards me and engulfed me in their game, jumping up and down with glee, chanting, *"oyinbo pepe, luku luku pepe!"*. My constant presence did nothing to dull the excitement of catching sight of the white woman. Then came the sound of Grace's voice calling me, "Ann, Ann, are you there? Come down and have some food, I've made you *egusi* soup, your favourite!"

They called me the one who had come there as a stranger, *alejo*, a visitor from somewhere far away, a white woman, the one they said whose pink skin was peeled, inside-out skin, the kind of skin you see when you cut yourself with a cutlass or rip open your foot on a stone. They'd given me the name Ajoke, the-one-everyone-wants-to-pet. I'd felt it then: a moment of perfect peace, a moment in which I – white woman, *alejo*, stranger – somehow belonged. I'd never felt so cared for before.

And now? I wasn't so sure. Everything suddenly felt a bit less solid, a bit less certain. My rational self railed against the impact of the herbalist's words and tried to summon back the level-headed sceptic. But doubt had crept in, and I was filled with a mounting sense of foreboding. Hadn't the herbalist had said to me that people were watching me, people who wanted to do harm? People who didn't want to see me succeeding? He'd asked me if I ever felt afraid. I'd retorted that I never felt frightened, that people in the town had taken me in as one of their own. He and Iya Dayo both looked sceptical.

"Iya Dayo," I said, keeping my voice low and even. "Can you take a look in that bag, and see what's in it? Is it a calabash?"

"No", Iya Dayo wrapped her arms ever more tightly around her body. "I don't want to touch it. I know what is in it. It is juju. That herbalist, he said to you that you had people watching you. And now you find this in your car." Her voice trailed off.

For all the appearance of devoutness she liked to exude, there was nothing Iya Dayo liked more than stories involving bad medicine and bad intentions. She was full of cautionary tales. She would listen with rapt attention as herbalists spun their tales, taking mental notes that she'd use later in retelling the tales to her friends after church. Today's conversation had already been filed away. But the unfolding story was rapidly becoming more than a playful tale of encounters with herbalists.

Out of the corner of my eye, I could see Iya Dayo had now unwrapped her arms and was folding and unfolding her hands on her knees. She had begun that low, under-the-breath muttering that came over her at odd moments. I realised that Iya Dayo was praying. Things must be serious.

"What should we do?" I asked. "I mean, what should we do with it?"

Suddenly I found myself shivering. The car crept forward. The passersby and stall holders had been transformed into crowds of strangers, people who might wish me ill. My eyes engaged those of a man dressed in a baby blue lace *agbada* and cap. The man shot me a glare, his eyes flashing with evident distaste, holding my eyes briefly before breaking the gaze and turning away. My body broke out in goose pimples; there was something in his eyes that pared me down to bare life. I felt them burning into me even as the car bore us away.

We drove in silence past a gaggle of children standing in the doorway of one of the mud plaster houses with rusting corrugated roofs that lined the main road. They were too busily absorbed in their games to notice the white woman's car passing by.

It was tempting to go straight to Margaret's place. For one thing, there was invariably a group of older men there who liked to think of themselves having the combined wisdom to deal with just about anything, especially after a few pints of Nigerian Guinness, a syrupy dark drink that bore only a passing resemblance to the brew served lukewarm in English pubs. But it was more Margaret herself, with her impatient pragmatism, that I had in mind.

She'd take the calabash, pull it out of the bag, and shake it, saying, "Anna, what did I tell you about going to all those herbalists? They're trouble. They will turn your head. Watch out, you will see it for yourself if you don't stop. I know you say this is your research, but can't you do something better with your time? Surely there must be other ways for you to do your studies."

She had given me that lecture a few times already, remonstrating with me, "It's just not good for you, going here and there in the hot sun asking too many questions."

Maybe not Margaret, not this time. Grace, that's who I need right now. Grace can sort this out.

We'd reached the motorpark next to our house. A scrawny dog lay in the shade, paw poised in mid-air as if to scratch another flea the moment it bit. A group of middle-aged men clustered in the half-built concrete shell next to the old mud plaster house, drinking palm wine and playing cards. I drew the car to a halt and jumped out. Iya Dayo sprang out after me and began crossing herself.

I made my way over to the men, greeting them before explaining what had happened. I pointed to the car, "and it's still there, on the dashboard. I don't know what to do." The men got to their feet and approached the car as if it had in it a ticking bomb about to go off. I opened the door, gesturing at the black plastic bag on the dashboard. All three of them jumped. It would have been comical if it had been funny. But it wasn't. It was deadly serious.

For a few seconds Iya Dayo, the three men and I stood frozen to the spot. No-one wanted to make the first move. Then there was a fast-moving clatter of heels and Grace came into view, dressed to the nines in her Lagos clothes: iridescent turquoise Guinea brocade, the kind of cloth Nigerian traders buy in bulk in London's Petticoat Lane to sell in Lagos' markets, strappy golden sandals, deep burgundy lipstick and a lightening foundation that made her face glimmer with an ethereal glow.

"What's going on here?" Grace demanded.

I told her, looking sheepish. Grace was with Margaret on the issue of my fascination with herbalists.

"Well, let's get it out of the car then," she pronounced. Grace marched over to the car, flung open the door and, crossing herself before she touched the black bag, picked it up with one hand and carried it, as if it were a bag full of excrement, and hurled it onto a nearby rubbish heap that was smouldering with the remains of last night's fire.

Everyone flinched. All eyes focused on the plastic bag, waiting for it to shrivel in the heat. But it was too far from the embers, and just lay there in its bed of ashes.

The men, who had retreated to the shade of a nearby tree, burst into raucous applause, shattering the silence. I descended into nervous laughter. Iya Dayo surreptitiously crossed herself once again and muttered a swift line of prayer.

Grace was on her way back indoors when a small boy with a close-shaven head and ragged shorts came running through the motorpark towards us.

"This your car?" he asked me, panting.

"Yes, how can I help you?" I said.

"My uncle needs to go to Ipokia. There's a masquerade. They've asked him to bring medicine. He told me to put the calabash in the brown 504 for him and he would follow me. But when he came out of my father's place and went to his car, he didn't find it there. They came to get me, and I saw that the car I'd put it in had gone."

Gasping to recover his breath, he recounted the rest of the tale. It turned out he'd asked the petty trader sitting by the roadside selling single sticks of cigarette, chewing gum and sweets if she'd seen anything. "The *oyinbo* took the car," she told him. He needed no further information: everyone knew where the white woman lived and traded on stories about whom she was and why she was there. I looked down at his bare feet. He'd run here, hoping that he could find the calabash for his uncle to take to Ipokia. Without it, the masquerade would have no power. The ritual would have no effect. The entire festival would grind to a halt.

It was an emergency.

"It's here. Don't worry." I smiled at the boy, gesturing at the black plastic bag sitting on top of a dusty pile of cartons, crisp wrappers, and half-burnt debris. I walked over and picked it up gingerly to hand it to him. The bag had not yet lost its power over me. I had to find a way of shaking off the fear that had crept over me. Sensing that Grace and Iya Dayo were going to round on me to pick over the afternoon's events and chastise me again for my unhealthy interest in herbalists, I turned to the boy.

"Look," I said. "Can I give you a lift back?"

He eyed me with astonishment. The *oyinbo*. Offering him a ride in her car. His face broke into a smile, his eyes dancing with delight. He nodded. Iya Dayo stood stock-still watching the scene, her face etched with a show of evident distaste as I opened the passenger door and ushered the boy inside.

Retracing my steps to Doctor Yinka's, I could not help eyeing the black plastic bag with the calabash bouncing harmlessly on the dashboard as I negotiated the potholes. And on my way back home, I made sure I caught the eyes and returned the smiles and waves of those who watched the *oyinbo* passing by for a second time that afternoon.

For all that I would always be an *alejo*, being Ajoke gave me a comfort I couldn't remember ever having felt before in my life: a warm feeling of being looked after, cared for. I held onto that feeling, carrying it with me into the mud plaster family house, letting it linger later that night as I closed my wooden shutter, tightened my mosquito net and eased myself into bed.

'FACE YOUR CHILDREN AND YOUR WORK'

Iya Dayo and I were sitting on the porch of a woman who lived close enough by for me to have heard the shouting coming from her house. She had confided in us that her husband used to beat her, especially after he'd had a few drinks. He'd keep her from pursuing her trade, saying he did not want her to go here and there because she might meet other men. That stopped her from going to the ring of markets around the town where she might have turned a better profit from her cloth business than she could from her porch, which is where he had her sequestered.

That day, she told us of how she'd found out that her husband had another woman. That he'd been sleeping with that woman for seven years, during which the woman had borne him two children. All of this under her nose. She had no idea it was going on. He'd tell her he was going to the farm, disappearing on an *okada* and coming back late in the night reeking of alcohol. She'd assumed he was drinking palm wine with the other men under the shade of the trees that lined their farm, as she'd seen them do in the late afternoon. But it turned out he was nowhere near the farm. He'd taken to visiting the area behind the mosque where the "women from Ghana" - as they were euphemistically called – lived. He'd became a regular of one of those women, and then he'd become her lover. Soon, he found himself being asked for money to feed the children she'd begun to bear for him. And the children were growing, the eldest one old enough for school.

That's how he was caught. The child passed through the town on the way back from school, dressed in green gingham shirt and forest green shorts. The spitting image of his father. As he wove

144

through the market, he passed a stall where the woman and her friends were sitting in the mid-afternoon lull. One of them said hey, that boy looks just like your husband. She called out to him. He stopped still in his tracks. They looked him up and down, then sent him on his way. Later that evening, she'd tackled her husband. It had all come out. The lies. Those long years of deceit. The shame of it all. And then he'd gone out and got drunk and come back and beaten her so badly that the side of her face was bruised and swollen.

"What about his mother or his sister?" I asked, "can't they do anything?"

She scoffed at the thought. "They're as bad as he is," she said, "they blame me for everything. Just yesterday they claimed I'd put something in the water to make everyone ill."

Piped water was still rare in the town. Many people kept water in large clay urns. Stories of people being poisoned by someone in the compound putting medicine in the water were legion.

Ehinkule l'ota wa, people would say. The enemy is inside the house.

I told her the story of my aunt, who found out one day that her husband had another woman in the town where he went to work every week. That man had kept the relationship with the other woman going for nine years without her finding out. When she discovered it, she was beside herself with fury and hurt. The betrayal, the lying, the indignity of it all.

The woman nodded. "It even happens in your country," she said quietly.

A heavy silence hung over us for a few minutes. Then she began to ask me more about it all.

"What of her parents? Did they find out?"

"Yes, my aunt was very close to her mother. She told her the whole story."

That ginger-haired bastard, I remembered my grandmother calling him at the time.

"But there was nothing that the parents could do. She'd left their house to get married to him," I said, "and in my country it is really unusual for someone to go back to their parents' house when they're an adult and have children of their own. In any case, her parents had moved into a smaller house, and she couldn't really live there with her children."

The woman nodded again, "yes that's what makes it hard here, if you go back there is shame, everyone asking what's happened, are you troublesome. Here, they call you *ilemosu* - the one who returns to their father's house without a good excuse - if you leave your husband's house and go home. They say you are stubborn, that you have brought it on yourself, that you are the kind of character who no-one would want to marry."

"And," she said, "no woman wants to leave her children behind. You can take them with you if they're small, but as soon as they're old enough to go to school the father's family will claim them as theirs. Then they can't stay with you again."

I'd heard heart-breaking stories of women who had been thrown out by their husbands or left because of violence whose children would secretly visit them, and the harsh treatment those children might expect from their father's new wives. Some years later, when I was asked in a job interview what policy changes I'd advocate on the basis of my research, the first thing that came to mind is a change in the custody laws. I was struck by the ambivalent coloniality in that very desire for a change in laws that owed their origin to the British colonial regime.

The British brought not only their mores, but also their contradictions. There were laws that were visited on the colonies as versions of what was in place at home, and others that had their origins in the colonies as the administrators grappled with their 'civilising' mission. Then there were customs and practices that the British hardened into law, along with the introduction of a system of courts that passed from being instruments of colonial rule to mechanisms for the reinforcement of local patriarchal preoccupations.

For many women, the idea of *packing out* before their children were safely settled in adult lives was unthinkable. The very idea of no longer being able to mother their children was just too monstrous. It was not just the emotional impact of not being able to see and care for their children. It spoke to the very unravelling of their identities as mothers. But there was more to it. Just like the trope of the evil stepmother British children are exposed to at a young age, in the traditional children's stories like Cinderella that have now become classic Disney animations, there was the lurking fear that if a woman did pack out and leave her children, who knows what might happen to them.

Women regaled me with the possible dangers their children would be exposed to if they were not there to shield and protect them. Beatings. And worse. Stories would circulate of stepmothers starving and even poisoning children from another mother, to advantage their own children's inheritance prospects. You never knew what kind of wife the husband you'd left would bring home to replace you. So, women told me, they just stuck it out. Husbands could be reduced to a minor annoyance. "You face your children and your work," they'd say.

"You know what happened?" I continued the story of my aunt. "She didn't leave him. She was so upset. But she had nowhere to go. She had no job. No money of her own. No house of her own. She took a good hard look at the situation and thought of what her life might be like if she left or threw him out. Her house, her status, the things she'd spent all those years on making her life – all of that would be gone."

The woman nodded again. Iya Dayo joined in. "It's better for women to endure, for the sake of the children. It's the children who will surely suffer if she doesn't."

I wasn't so sure about this business of endurance. But I could see how resigning yourself to facing your children and your work might at least mean women could find a bit of peace in troubled relationship. I'd seen my own mother do this. And many years later I'd find myself doing the same, at least for a while.

THE GOOD HUSBAND

Iya Dayo and I were wandering rather aimlessly through Imasai Quarter one hot afternoon. We'd spent the morning crammed inside a low roofed mud plaster meeting hall of one of the apostolic churches, as supplicants howled their prayers. Iya Dayo took great pleasure in such outings. She'd hum to herself for some hours afterwards, noting down particularly resonant prayer phrases in the little book she carried with her.

I would emerge from these occasions irritable and rebellious, ready to pick a fight with anyone who tried to convince me that it wasn't all just a way to fleece people of scarce resources. These pastors would peddle the gospel of prosperity. People would make a down payment, anticipating a return as their prayers were answered; the pastor would pocket it, accumulating the money to build lavish homes and drive the glitziest Mercedes-Benz. Rather than evidence of corruption, this would be interpreted as a sign of the power of the prayers he was able to channel.

In my view, there was a simple term for all this: 419, the article in the Nigerian criminal code relating to the scamming practice that came to be known internationally as extracting money from people with the promise of lucre in return.

I knew better than to strike up a conversation with Iya Dayo when I was in this kind of mood. Anthropologists are supposed to keep their opinions to themselves. I needed to contain myself from being plain rude. We walked in silence, through narrow beaten red mud paths between houses with their rusted corrugated iron roofs and terracotta mud plaster walls. Occasionally, a child shouted "*Oyinbo, Oyinbo!*". Sometimes they would dash up close just to steal a peek at the white woman wending her way through the neighbourhood, and I'd smile, and we'd play, giggling delightedly together.

"This", I told Iya Dayo, "is why I don't want to drive everywhere". She looked at me, uncomprehending. Why, when I had a car, were we not using it? She didn't much like this meandering. It was baking hot. People had retreated to the cool of darkened rooms in their compounds. It was hard to strike up a casual chat.

When we came across a woman sitting in her doorway weaving a mat, I almost just greeted her with that exchange of formalities extended to strangers within a certain vicinity and walked on.

"*Ẹ ku ikale, Ma,*" I called, with the greeting used for someone who is sitting.

Then I spied a big metal bowl and a pile of plastic jerrycans by the side of the house, signs that she might be one of those soda soap makers I'd seen in the market.

"Shall we stop and talk with her?" I asked Iya Dayo.

With a visible sigh, Iya Dayo stopped walking and turned towards the woman. This was the consequence of us meandering. I'd randomly want to chat to strangers and ask them all manner of questions.

My whiteness gave me a certain kind of license, and I knew that. It also gave me liabilities. The curse of hyper-visibility. The swarm of suppositions about who I was and what I was doing that buzzed noisily around me as I moved through the town. Spy, missionary, oddball. Was my skin really peeled inside out like some people said it was and that was why I was so pink, and sometimes red from the sun and the heat? Why was it so hard to understand it when I spoke?

I greeted her first for the afternoon and then asked after her health and that of her family. She nodded and thanked me with a soft spoken *adupe* after every step in the chain of greetings, until I stopped, smiling awkwardly as I waited for Iya Dayo to come in and ask if we could ask her some questions. Nodding, she gestured to a couple of white plastic chairs at the entrance to the dark hallway with a polished concrete floor that led into the bowels of the house. I hauled them outside, arranging them around her so as to avoid the narrow path that ran along the outside of her house.

I imagined what might be running through the woman's mind as she sat there in a boldly patterned burgundy, green and yellow *buba* and wrapper, her head tie pushed back and her forehead bristling with beads of mid-afternoon sweat.

Where to begin? With the metal bowl, I thought; it was propped up against the side of the house, with dusty yellow jerrycans beside it that looked as if they'd been there for a while. I went through the ritual of explaining that I'd never quite managed to get right. *I am a student from Britain and I am studying women's lives. I am from London and my university sent me to Nigeria to learn. I am from England and I am learning about life in Nigeria for my studies.* It didn't really stack up.

Undeterred, I asked Iya Dayo to introduce me and ask permission for me to write her answers down, explaining that it would be part of an assignment I was writing for my studies.

"Tell her that I'm studying women's work", I said. "To find out about how this current economic situation in Nigeria is affecting women."

The words were barely off Iya Dayo's lips before the woman began talking, a long, emotional, stream of narrative wending its way between us.

"She said that things are hard these days," Iya Dayo said.

"Tell me what exactly she said," I implored, "she seemed to be saying more than this."

I cursed again the fact that my Yoruba was so poor that I could only pick up occasional words. I'd heard 'soap', 'goose', *'bata'* (shoes), 'husband'. My curiosity was piqued. The woman began talking again, and this time, Iya Dayo translated, patiently, stopping the woman from time to time to give her a breather.

I sat there scribbling away in my notebook, greedy for all the details. It was a tale with elements that were so unusual that I wanted to catch every word. A supportive husband. A husband with ambitions for his wife and with spare cash to keep on investing in her business ventures, time after time after time.

Shyly at first, she'd told us that when she'd first met her current husband, she wasn't sure what to make of him. She'd come to recognise, she said, that she needed a director in life, and he was the one. She was wife number four for him; a string of disastrous marriages, one after the next, had left him bruised. They found in each other, she said, something neither of them had expected or imagined possible. An easy relationship. And it was this husband, her director, who had given her the idea for the trade she'd been doing ever since: *bata*, shoes, which she got in bulk from Lagos and then sold from door to door in the quarter.

She gestured at the metal bowl. It was, it turned out, from a failed venture some years ago. She'd tried making soda soap, but first a duck fell into the mixture and died. "It was my husband's duck, so it was no matter," she said. But then she kept on getting the caustic soda mixture into her eyes. It wasn't for her. We fell to talking about how hard the times had become. Her story about the misadventure with the duck was like an apocryphal tale of the trials and tribulations of austerity.

It got me thinking about what it meant to be a trader in such uncertain times. There was a sense of impermanence that had come to colour everyday life. It went beyond the capriciousness of living in a situation marked by economic risk and myriad other forms of uncertainty. Insecurity bit into the social in unexpected ways. There was the hazard that people around you would take against you. Or, worse, that they would become quietly offended without you quite realising what it was that you'd done. And that there would be *trouble* that would spill over into your efforts to stay afloat economically.

I was constantly hearing stories about women who'd been brought to their knees and left in grinding poverty by fractured social relations, people defaulting on or denying them credit, the loss of their small stashes of capital due to perished or thieved goods, accidents that ended up with expensive medical bills. So much of this was ascribed to malevolent and ultimately unknowable intentions of others, to witchcraft, *juju*, bad people.

I thought about how hard it must be in a situation like this to anticipate how things might unfold when you took the plunge and started up a business or took a relationship to the next stage and set up home together. I'd read an article that described women's reproductive lives as 'careers'. The author had gone on to suggest that women made deliberate decisions, likened to 'career choices', in finding fathers for their children to secure themselves lines of economic sustenance even in the absence of any emotional connection.

Mulling over this, I thought it was plausible if you took a birds-eye view of their behaviour and worked back from the children they'd ended up having. But there was something about assuming this kind of cool rationality that just didn't feel right to me. I'd met loads of women who'd ended up having children with men they were seeing without intending to do so.

"The next thing is pregnancy", Iya Dayo would intone as

she talked about young women having affairs, with evident disapproval.

And that was the point. A chain of consequences may have nothing at all to do with having any particular sense of where things might go, let alone a deliberate set of choices weighed over and made. That's something about the human condition that gets missed when we treat people as if they're calculating each step they take from a position of being able to control which direction the next step will take them.

Often, it's just not the case. We might make sense of the things we did after they happened, telling ourselves and others a story that writes in intention, purpose, explanation. But much of the time we're just muddling through, figuring things out as we go.

It's curious to be researching coping with uncertainty in a situation where you yourself have got no plan and no real sense of what you're doing, but you carry on doing, just in case that *doing* turns into a *plan* that gathers some sense of purpose. I was *being* in Nigeria. I was *doing* the everyday things that I thought an anthropologist should be doing, as best as I knew how. I still didn't really know what would come of it.

Day by day, I'd go here and there in the town with Iya Dayo chatting to people, finding out new things, hearing and telling stories. My days would be full of a kind of social interaction that soon came to be a way of being in itself, sparse in the question-asking, relaxed in the listening. And people liked to talk. They'd invite us back, call us over when we were wandering through the narrow lanes of the town, treat our visits like an occasion that called for sending a child to the market to source warm Coke and Fanta for the guests. Maybe this was enough. Just being *was* doing. I kept writing everything down, compulsively, and combing through my notebooks for patterns, themes, story-lines, new questions.

I wanted what I wrote to be as real an account of lives lived in this town as it could be, not some kind of alienated pseudo-scientific study nor a mere catalogue of customs and practices, written without feeling. Love, respect, dignity, care. I wanted all of that to be in the way I represented people's lives and in the stories that I chose to tell. I wanted to imbue my writing with that feeling of shared humanity, for that to become the connecting thread through it all, even when the differences between us seemed so significant it was hard to find anything in between. I came to see this as the most important work of the kind of anthropologist I'd like to be, one whose text evokes what it is to be human.

But all this was wishful thinking. It got me no closer to what I was going to do with all those pages of closely written, blue carbon copied, numbered pages of fieldnotes. I was still busy opening new lines of enquiry and filling up my record books. I'd got to F. Before I had so much as begun filling the first pages of G, I'd begun a detour that took me in a quite unexpected direction.

TO BE A MAN IS MORE THAN A DAY'S WORK

"She became a man," Iya Babutunde explained, finishing up a long and complicated story about a trader who'd become so wealthy, she was able to influence the politics of the town. We were sitting on her porch, surrounded by baskets of kola nuts. She sat on a low stool, a basket between her legs, picking through the kola. Her brown and cream patterned head-tie was pushed back from her forehead, which she wiped from time to time with the back of her hand. Iya Dayo nodded, approvingly. "Oh yes. That woman. She could do and undo." I liked the idea of that: a woman so powerful as to be seen as someone who could *do and undo*.

The conversation left me intrigued. What did a woman need to do to become a man? Could a man become a woman? How did gender and power play out to make such transitions possible? I'd read the provocative argument by Oyèrónké Oyěwùmí that suggested that Yorubas didn't do gender until the colonisers squeezed everyone into the straight jacket of their binary. But I wasn't completely convinced. Yoruba is a gender-free language. Yet I'd heard certain attributions used to evoke differences that made use of gendered language. Like the description I was given of the kind of fibroids that really hurt versus the small ones that you have without even knowing. The male variety was the one to cause pain. No surprises there.

155

For weeks, I'd been faithfully cataloguing women's economic activities. But there wasn't yet a story line in it. I could present a picture of the different occupations available to women. I could describe how to bargain for a tomato and how it's different to bargaining for a jerry can of palm oil or a 6m bale of imported printed cloth. I could present extended case studies of women's trading careers. Like Iya Galura, who'd started gathering sticks from farms and head-loading them to town to sell as firewood, who'd lost her trading capital to creditors as she tried to switch trades, and then who'd settled on the love of her life, the strong coloured dyes used to stain the reeds older women used to make mats, *galura*. Iya Galura rose to enjoy wealth and stature, her house full of adopted children given to her by relatives to raise as she had no children of her own. Had she become a man?

I knew of other women who were influential in the town. One was leader of the largest association of Muslim women and also the Iyalode, the head of the market. She'd come to our house in the evening to talk politics with an earnest group of the town's male elders, the only woman in the room. I'd spent time with her, finding out about her life. She was the first to tell me of something I came to hear again and again from older women, a scenario that younger women burdened by a useless or violent husband would evoke as a future possibility that could give them reprieve. A room of their own. Waiting until her children were grown up and married, she "packed out" into a two-story house that she'd built for herself in one of the more desirable neighbourhoods of the town. She'd bought it little by little, first the land and then, with the proceeds of each month's profits, building one storey and then the next.

"Did you ever think of getting married again?" I asked her.

She roared with laughter. "Married?! I went to the battle front and came back. Enough is enough".

She was now able to 'do and undo'. Had she become a man?

I thought back to the hours I'd spent in the local customary court, combing through the records. I would never have thought about looking there had it not been for a session given to an eager class of would-be anthropologists by one of our most distinguished professors of African History. I associated courts with trials and judgements. But he enlightened us. What happens in a court is painstakingly recorded. Statements are taken verbatim. Judgements are transcribed. Breaches in the law and cases for the prosecution and defence reveal social norms and mores. All of this is encoded in longhand and preserved for the historical record. It was a treasure trove. The cases were at times performative, at others perfunctory. But they contained rich evidence of what it was to be a man, a woman, a husband, a wife.

Suddenly, it felt as if I was on to something.

I had an idea. I'd become a bit more adventurous with my methods. My interviewing style had become very loose. It was easy enough, I found, to pursue paths of enquiry if the person I was interviewing was getting something out of it. Not for me the barrage of questions that I associated with interview protocols, with all their formality. I wanted people to enjoy talking to me, rather than sit in stiff anticipation waiting for the next question. I wanted our conversations to be open-ended, fluid, curious, reflective. I wanted them to be spaces where we could ruminate, together, about the stuff that mattered in life. Interviews should, I thought, punctuate a busy day in a way that would give something back to the people who'd so generously given their time. Could we turn the work of the interview into something more enjoyable and useful for participants? Create conversations that were restorative? Relaxing? What were the rules? How much could an interview be like a chat? A coaching session? A counselling session?

This thought experiment snowballed, as ethics became entangled with methodology. How would this way of working affect what counted as 'data'? What were the boundaries that determined which secrets could be safely secreted and which could become material to be woven into what I would write – that is, as soon as I'd figured out what my thesis would be about? What does consent amount to in such a situation? How does an anthropologist explain what they're going to take away from an interaction if the headnotes they're making only end up being written down many months later? And what kinds of interactions are within and off limits in participant observation?

So many questions. All of them took me circling back to the bigger ethical question of what business I had, as a white British person, to be poking around in people's private lives looking for stories. The disquiet of the coloniality of it all was like nausea; present at a low level most of the time, sometimes becoming so intense that I literally felt sick. But I also chastised myself for taking it all so seriously, making it all matter so much: there was also something problematic in that, it felt like a kind of self-indulgence. I remembered how irritated I'd felt at the level of navel-gazing going on in anthropology at the time. Surely these people's introspection isn't doing anything for the people they're working with, the students they're educating. Where's the politics in it?

I began thinking differently about what I was doing. I'd been increasingly self-conscious about wasting people's time with my questions. I was caught in the loop of worrying that I was guilty of exoticizing the everyday, in a way that only anthropologists can. Malinowski, founding father of fieldwork, complained in a piece written in 1930 called "Practical Anthropology" that anthropologists are preoccupied by what he called 'sensational or antiquarian interests... the explanation of customs which appear to us strange, quaint, incomprehensible' rather than with 'the broad and bigger problems of anthropology'.[4]

It was one of those 'broad and bigger problems' that I was interested in: what it means to be human. I took to approaching the task of finding out differently, building on the direction I'd been taking in open-ended interviewing. I began not with a list of questions that I wanted to ask people, but with openings that invited a conversation that meandered in whatever direction the speaker wanted to take it. This often took us into stories from the person's lived experience and their reflections on the past and the present, a bit like a life history but led more by their narrative than my interests. My questions became the gentle prompts of a listener intrigued by what I was hearing, playing back bits of it to check I'd understood properly but also to show that I really was paying attention. I later found out this way of listening had a method associated with it: the Biographic-Narrative Interpretive Method.[5]

In an intensely industrious culture, having time just to sit around and chat is a luxury. It was one that I came to associate with older men, who would happily enough draw me into conversation in the shadow of their porches in the long hot afternoon sun. They'd tell me life stories that traced the contours of colonial rule, from the classrooms in the mission schools in town, to life in the city where they'd worked as clerks and trades people. Their stories painted a post-colonial landscape in which young men were able invent futures for themselves that were markedly different to the pasts their fathers had lived through.

At first, I thought it would put people off to have me writing everything down. But it was quite the opposite. There was something that I came to see as validation in taking a written account of what I was being told. When I turned up without my notebook, I was asked where it was. The idea that words were there for the record, that I was recording life, all of that seemed much more explicable than just rocking up and 'hanging out' and then writing up whatever I could remember afterwards in my fieldnotes, as I had been told I ought to do.

It also felt more honest. People told me stuff. I wrote it down. They could see me filling the pages of my notebook in front of them. I still used my fieldnotes to capture things that had happened, incidents, snatches of conversation, reflections. More and more, my 'data' became these transcripts of on-the-record conversations rather than the fieldnotes I carried on writing up every evening, capturing the impressions and events of the day.

I hadn't expected to be thanked by the people I interviewed; it was me who was grateful to them for their time, I'd say, humbled and embarrassed by their thanks. When it kept on happening, I began to reflect on that act of attentive listening, following the flow of the speaker and speaking only to prompt them to continue. I came to see it as creating a kind of reflective space, one that could also be affirming. My whiteness gave me the power, in those moments, to verbalise recognition of the adversity women had experienced, their struggles, their moments of joy and satisfaction. And when the interviews became dialogues, as they so often did, they affirmed our shared humanity as often as they enabled reflection on our differences.

I wasn't just listening more. I was also telling different stories. After my initial finding-out interviews and my brief excursion into telling feminist fables to provoke a response, I'd started to tell tales that got to the fact that beneath the more obvious differences between us, there was much that we had in common. The American anthropologist Ruth Benedict gave a meaning to the discipline that went beyond the cataloguing of cultures when she said, 'the purpose of anthropology is to make the world safe for human differences'.

Could practising anthropology have the purpose, I wondered, of bringing to us more of an awareness of our shared humanity, in all its glorious diversity? Not just in helping us to understand what it means to be human, but as a way of *being human*?

TROUBLE IN
THE HOUSE

"*Obinrin iku aiye!*" exclaimed Iya Dayo. It was a saying she used often. *Women are the death of the world.* "Look at the trouble we're hearing about. Daily," she retorted. "The woman who tried to poison the child of her husband's other wife. The one who caused the husband to send that young woman back to her father's house. And that one who was running here and there after men while her husband was working in Lagos."

Men, in Iya Dayo's reckoning, were simply pawns in women's games with each other. She'd butter them up, indulging them. But it seemed to me that like many women, she lacked much confidence in their capabilities. Quick to assert men's prerogative, especially when I'd launched into one of my feminist fables, Iya Dayo took no time in denouncing their failings.

All around me, I heard complaints of 'useless men'. What does it mean to be a 'useless man', I wondered. What does it take to be described as 'useless'? Amongst the brightly coloured car stickers and mottos painted on the wooden slats on the back of older lorries, there were slogans that spoke of ideals of masculinity. *To Be a Man is More Than a Day's Work*, said one, a reminder that manhood was a state under construction. *Downfall of a Man is Not the End of his Life* was a poignant reminder; should it happen, there's at least some kind of reprieve.

What drew me to Nigeria was the prospect of being in a society where women's power was treated with awe, feared and celebrated. I was hearing about women who became so economically and politically powerful they *became men*. But also about men who failed to live up to what was expected of them and were described as *useless*. These were not simple binaries.

There seemed to be something else going on.

On the one hand, there were clear expectations of men and women - ones that were being breached. Anthropologists attend to what is being said, as well as what isn't. When something is said a lot, by lots of different people, then you're onto something; it becomes worth investigating.

Why, I wondered, was there what seemed to be almost a moral panic going on? It was clearly linked to the economic situation, but there was something else about it that intrigued me. The talk wasn't just about men or about women. It was about men as (failed) husbands. And - at least in the case of the girls who were accused of 'uselessing themselves' – it was about women in what 'Molara Ogundipe-Leslie described as the 'coital and conjugal' roles that African women, in all their complexity, were so often reduced to in writings by people like me.

I'd been getting to find out about all that complexity. But I kept coming back to that question of disappointed expectations.

The *useless man* was a man who failed to be of use. He was someone who wasn't willing or able to provide for his family, either because he was incapable of making a living or unable to stop squandering his money. I looked around at the men I'd got to know. I reckoned there were few amongst them who could be labelled in this way. But I knew one or two.

The one to whom I was closest was a sweet man who loved his kids to bits. He confided in me once that he'd joined the army because he'd been bullied at school for not being tough enough. Once he'd found himself in the armed forces being toughened up, the bullying got worse. Sanctioned from above, sustained by all around him, the kind of bullying he'd experienced was one that kept a very particular version of being a man in close focus. And he was useless at all of that. Really useless. He stepped away, came back and never really found what it was that he was good for.

That was, at least, his version of himself. From this, he took to drink. Strong, cheap liquor called *ogogoro,* a word that sounds like what happens to you when you become blotto after drinking it all afternoon under the shade of a tree or in a small band of fellow male fugitives from expectation in the hours when women busy themselves preparing dinner and corralling their children.

Drink emboldened. It also absorbed the emotions that uselessness left him with; anger, hurt, a sense of hopelessness about the future. His wife was one of those women who threw back the small notes he might timorously offer her, saying "how now?" and wondering, loudly, what was to be done to feed her and her children with such paltry offerings. She reputedly had another lover, a businessman who plied his prospering trade in a nearby market town. It was whispered that she'd been seen disappearing into the back of his shop more than a few times, emerging some while later bathed in the aftermath of stolen moments of pleasure.

To be a man in these times was more than a day's work. It was a real struggle. Some men flipped and resorted to violence, as well as to drink. Anthropologists have talked of this violence in terms of men feeling *thwarted,* cheated of the entitlements of their masculinity, the promises of power that they'd been brought up believing would be theirs until they realised that they weren't going to have any of this. I'd read this way of explaining things with curiosity. Could it really be the case that male violence could be attributed so directly to men not being able to access the means from which to make their masculine ideals?

Women told me that in the past, the elders in the compound would take a man aside and give him a roasting if he beat his wife unduly harshly and *without a good reason.* What, I enquired, was a good reason? Quite a few were offered in response. Not getting food ready on time featured high on the list. The rest were about being pliable enough to accommodate whatever the men required of their wives.

How did men get to feel they could get away with it, especially if they were not fulfilling their part of the bargain and providing their wives and families with *chop money* – money to buy food? And why did these economically empowered women stand for it? Because, I realised, of the same things that stopped anyone in my family telling anyone about my father, who would drink and drink and then become enraged at the slightest infraction, triggering long nights of beatings, shouting and threats. We weren't labelled as those experiencing the thing that development agencies came to call VAWG, Violence Against Women and Girls. White and middle-class as we were, we also lived in fear. Like the women who told me that they 'face their children and their work', my mother *endured*.

'Useless' seemed a word that captured a present reality that was far from ideal, for men as well as women. But what about the past? Was there a time in which husbands did live up to expectations that women had of them? I wondered to what extent these expectations had been shaped by the same kinds of social forces that had created an identity as wife for my mother in the 1950s, which she battled to free herself from as the 1980s took shape and women began to realise that they had options.

I'd met an American historian in Ibadan, Lisa Lindsay, who was asking these questions. As her research developed, the answers she came up with brought an unexpected dimension to the story of what it meant to be a husband in southern Nigeria. The ideal of the husband as breadwinner was, she pointed out, a relatively recent invention. Looking back, it should have stood to reason. It was such a very Victorian construction of what marriage was all about, one that had lingered in the UK until my mother's generation had begun to contest it. So many British men still labour under its constraints and treat themselves to its prerogatives. So many British women submit to its benefits and suffer its limitations.

I took to asking people: "if you were born again and were able to choose whether you were a man or a woman, what would you choose?" Most chose to be men and their versions of what it was to be a man, circled again around what it meant to be a *husband*. Bimpe, an unmarried woman in her early 20s, gave "being in control" as her reason for wanting to be a man. Peter, in his 50s, said he wouldn't want to be a woman as the man would be dominating him all the time: "Men usually command women as they like, if they want them to do anything, if they don't want them to go out anywhere, they can stop them from going. Women are under the husband's control for as long as they are in the house." Bola, in her 30s, put it even more directly. She'd be a man, she said, and would marry many wives. Then she would just sit in her chair ordering her wives around: "Get me this! Get me that!" And Bose, a teenager, concurred. She would marry many wives, she said - and beat them thoroughly if they didn't obey her.

For men and women alike, it wasn't just being a man. It was being a Husband. This meant being vested with control over the household. I recalled reading Ifi Amadiume's book *Male Daughters, Female Husbands* and the revelation that it offered: husband was a role, as well as a relationship. It was one that could be taken by women, and not just in lesbian or queer relationships. That role - the provider, the protector, the head of the family - was something that men were really struggling with as the economic crisis bit. But it was also something that felt as if it represented a normative ideal coming from somewhere else, to which people felt they needed to measure themselves and others.

I observed how some men talked, as they affirmed their desire to be reborn as men, about the challenges of living up to the ideals they described. One spoke of how men can't control women. Another said, "Men don't like women to earn more than them as the women may then refuse their orders." Another mused on how he'd like to be a *real man*, stronger, able to work really hard.

Women's versions of husband, voiced not in idealised statements but in everyday complaints, were different. Good husbands, rare as they seemed to be, were men who took their responsibilities seriously, rather than those who used their rights to enforce control. One woman in her 40s complained: "In the olden days, the husband was responsible for everything. But now you're lucky if he gives half. That's why women are running here and there trying to make money." And one woman in her 50s grumbled, "In Nigeria, there are no husbands anymore. No men are catering properly for their wives and children."

All this talk about husbands got me thinking. What was being naturalised here? Felicia Ekejiuba's work introduced me to the idea of the *hearth-hold* as a replacement for the flawed idea of 'household' that revolved around a man as head. The concept of hearth-hold centres women's industry and nurturance of their families; men might be part of hearth-holds, but be quite peripheral in women's everyday lives, especially if they weren't making much of a contribution.

I started unpacking the version of gender relations that I'd internalised because it was one that came from my own culture, imported and imposed on this one. In its place, I put 'Molara Ogundipe-Leslie's STIWANISM and her insistence on locating African women and men within a broader context of the impact of colonial and neocolonial structures of oppression. These structures, she argues, place African men above women in social hierarchies. African womens' struggles, she argues, are shaped by the endorsement of patriarchal values that they have themselves internalised.

It all started to make sense.

MAKING SENSE

There's a belief amongst anthropologists that you can't become one without doing fieldwork; there's literally nothing that can substitute for what you learn by immersing yourself in a different culture and emerging with an account of why things work and why people are the way they are in that context. Those moments of abject strangeness dissolve through a gentle immersion that slowly, almost imperceptibly, brings you to a place where you're starting to dream, think, feel, and react differently.

The craft of the anthropologist lies not only in the interactions that provide 'data'. It is also in choosing which fragments of information to transpose into fieldnotes or encode in transcripts of conversations that are close enough to what was said for them to be used, verbatim, later. And it's in sifting through the closely written pages, remembered snatches of conversation, sights and smells, little reminders written on scraps of paper, that anthropologists piece it all together to tell a story that sheds light and gives meaning.

This order-making, this pattern-finding, is a slow process. It's one of the reasons why anthropological fieldwork takes so long. Most anthropologists spend at least a year in the field; some spend most of their lives going back and forth from classroom to fieldsite or poring over fieldnotes made decades before to pull out new nuggets of information or finally write up materials earlier overlooked into articles that take the latest concepts and apply them to *their* people.

Anthropologists make much of their fieldnotes. They're the place where they encode daily observations, snatches of dialogue, concepts they have come across, ideas that have come to them over the course of the day, how they think others are behaving and how they themselves are feeling. An anthropologist's fieldnotes tell their own stories. They capture the preoccupations of their writers, what's going on in their minds, what's puzzling or perplexing them, what they've discovered. But it is, as American anthropologist Roger Sanjek so memorably put it, 'headnotes' that most of us draw on when forming our accounts of whatever it is that we are studying.

Initial impressions are lodged in script, but also in mental images, feelings, smells, a multi-layered repository of stuff that can later be drawn upon in constructing text. And it's in that process of making text, weaving together all those pieces of information – sensory, remembered, recorded, inferred, heard – that ethnography is made. It's quite a laborious thing, doing anthropological research. You develop a heightened attentiveness to people and the things they do that's hard to switch off. But it also becomes one of the most valuable resources for living: there's literally never a dull moment for an anthropologist as long as there are people around to observe.

How does an anthropologist know? How do we get to a point where we think, yes, *now* I understand what's going in people's heads and why people do or say particular things? What does it take to be able to wear the mantle of ethnographic authority and pronounce on what people in a faraway place might think, feel, or say in reaction to the topic under discussion? Is it bluster? Academic arrogance? The blithe confidence of the pseudo-scientific neo-colonial? Or is there something in that process of immersion in another culture that really does allow you to learn about a people like you would a language, so much so that you become fluent?

I started tracing in my mind the times when I'd stumbled across something so utterly unexpected that it stopped me in my tracks. Was that where the learning lay: in those moments of recognition of utter difference?

Like the time a young woman came to the back door of our house in the late dusk hour when the centre of the town fell into a frenzy of movement, the roads lined with tiny flickering paraffin lamps of vendors selling snacks for the evening meal, lurching towards us out of the gloom with a small bundle on her back. She exchanged a few terse words with Grace, turned and walked away.

"What did she want?" I asked.

"That woman, she's going from house to house looking for someone to help her to bury her baby," Grace replied.

She'd been wandering around like this for days, it seemed, trying to find someone to intercede to persuade her husband's family to bury their child.

I could make out the figure of the woman disappearing into the gathering dusk. My heart went out to her. The little bump on her back was completely enclosed in a piece of what they called Java, the Dutch-made printed cloth sold in 6m lengths in the market. *She was walking around with a dead baby on her back.* I couldn't quite take it in. My mind sprang to a macabre sequence of images. I imagined picking up the tiny, pale, stiff, corpse and wrapping it in cloth to bind to your back, and how long it would take in this intense heat for the baby's little body to begin to decompose, the warm stench of rotting flesh trailing in her wake.

I grappled with trying to make sense of it. It hit me on so many levels. The raw immediacy of emotion in imagining what it must have felt like to wander around for days in a cloud of grief going to house after house in a desperate quest for intercession. The puzzle of the story that accompanied her that told of a woman who had been seen by the family as nothing but trouble, so now they were refusing to bury the baby she had borne their son. That son, refusing to acknowledge his child. And with it, the bond with the mother that had been so cruelly broken by the baby's death.

It got me thinking about what it meant to be a mother. To carry a child, feeling the first flutter inside you, like a little butterfly pupa in its chrysalis, growing the beginning of wings, brushing your insides so gently that it's barely perceptible. That incredible sensation when the baby is all restless movement, elbows and heels poking taut belly. Seeing and hearing their heartbeat in scans, recognising the little person growing inside you. I remember seeing my daughter Kate on the screen at the clinic for the first time, her hands folded behind her head and her ankles crossed, supine; an early glimpse of the baby-person who later emerged to greet the world, supremely chilled.

As an anthropologist, I could take that strangeness and connect with it as lived experience. Or I could treat it as something curiously Other, to be inspected and interrogated for what it might offer me in terms of nuggets of anthropological insight or instances of a particular concept or theory that I wanted to propound. So much of what I'd read when studying anthropology was strangely distanced from the raw feelings of desperate sadness that that woman with the dead baby brought up in me.

Even in moments of estrangement, when things seemed really very odd indeed, there was always something that brought me back to thinking about the human condition as something that connects us. Few anthropologists have been brave enough to tackle this directly. Nancy Scheper-Hughes' account of women who directed their mothering towards children more likely to survive, in *Death Without Weeping*. Renato Rosaldo's account of the fury of loss, *Grief and the Headhunter's Rage*. Ruth Behar's *The Vulnerable Observer*, in which she argues that the anthropologist should never become so detached that they can't connect with their own emotions in fieldwork. The book I'd return to like an old friend because it spoke to me with the familiarity of a kindred spirit, Michael Jackson's *Paths through a Clearing* starts with a reminder that the sense we make of the chaos of the world around us is a mechanism for staying sane; the order we bring to the otherwise random nature of the things that happen around us is part of what it means to be human.

While none arrested my thoughts and gripped my feelings in quite such a visceral way, there were other moments of utter strangeness. I wondered if the very disconnect between the way I made sense of things and what I was hearing from others meant that we lived in what were effectively parallel worlds. This is what was later to be called anthropology's 'ontological turn'. In those days the only turn in town was the 'reflexive turn'. It was being reflexive that got me thinking about the nature of being, with its complicated-sounding name, ontology.

There was an older anthropology that would explain things away, giving them a function and a place in the order of things. It was called Functionalism. Then there was Structural Functionalism, a quest to understand the functions of social structures. Then along came an anthropology that looked for the underlying rules that ordered the world, stripping myths and legends of their story-making qualities to boil them down to a set of principles that provide a script for living. It was called Structuralism. And it was followed by Post-Structuralism, which took everything apart and inspected it for its effects in sustaining regimes of power and knowledge. Then the Reflexive Turn. This is as far as it had got by the time I went to Nigeria. There were to be many more turns, the Affective Turn, the Post-Humanist Turn, the Seditious Turn.

I wondered what the people behind all these turns would have made of the story of the Tortoise Birth. Almost as far-fetched as the Virgin Birth, it was something that the adherents of the Ontological Turn would have made a right meal of, if they'd been the ones to describe it in their ethnographies. Proponents of the Reflexive Turn would have agonised over writing about it. Those of the Affective Turn would have empathised with the mother of the tortoise. Post-humanists would have had a field day. And as for the merry band of anthropologists proclaiming a Seditious Turn, they'd have used it as a metaphor for the exclusionary normativity of the discipline as a whole.

But at that stage, I didn't know about any of those turns. I was just trying to do ethnography. Iya Dayo and I had paid a visit to one of the many Pentecostal prophets who had set up shop in the town to bank on the rising popularity of the gospel of prosperity. He'd began spinning tales wilder than anything I'd heard from any of the herbalists. He told us of a woman in his congregation who had been pregnant for a very long time. Nine years. It was a condition known as *omo pe*, literally 'child is late'. It could be caused, people told me, by witches pressing down on a pregnancy so that it doesn't develop. Sometimes you couldn't even see it. Sometimes you could; the woman appears to have a ripening belly, but the baby doesn't arrive.

"Those women go here and there," Iya Dayo told me. "Looking for prayers, visiting herbalists."

That woman had been doing the same, by all accounts. That's how she ended up at his church. He took one look at her and knew that it was the work of the devil, he said. There was only one thing for it. She needed to come to stay in the church where she could be properly prayed over, so that the devil would leave her alone and the baby could be born. The woman was no doubt required to part with a hefty fee for the privilege. She moved into the church, and lived there with the prophet and his wives. They prayed for her several times a day, bathing her in holy water and feeding her special food brought by supplicants.

Slowly the pregnancy made itself seen. One day, not long afterwards, she went into labour. "It was the devil's work!" he said. She'd given birth to a tortoise, which they'd stared at dumbly as it wandered out of the church. The devil had got the better of her.

I found myself intellectualising, trying to solve the puzzle they presented me with as a good anthropologist ought to do. The thought struck me: what if in what I was noticing and noting there was an order or meaning that simply didn't exist in the minds of the people who I was observing? What if it was just my mind finding these patterns when someone else would find none, or different patterns?

How would I use stories like these? There's a politics to this when you're a white anthropologist reporting on Africa that goes beyond the narrative challenge of finding the stories that might grab your reader or help you make your point. Many of these stories also sat heavily with me as a feminist. My discomfort with Iya Dayo's moralising lectures had driven me to disagreeing with her in a very unanthropological way. And I'd noticed how differently I reacted when beliefs were shared with me about the nature of female malevolence and the prevalence of hatred; they evoked in me a sadness that was altogether more poignant. All this suggested the inevitability of women's frictions with each other as they lived, worked, and struggled in such close proximity.

These weren't stories that I wanted to have to tell. This is a real dilemma for the anthropologist when they're 'writing up': choosing which stories to tell and which remain closeted in the copiousness of what gets recorded or put aside because they're difficult to think or feel with. Does the ethnographer pick the stories that best illustrate what they're wanting to prove, in a twist to the method of having a hypothesis and testing it out to prove or disprove it? Or do those stories get treated on an equal footing, each one being carefully considered, sifted, weighed for its value? And when certain ones get told and others judged as not being telling enough, what truths are being constructed with them?

I realised that what had irritated me about the white American men whose angst filled the pages of *Writing Culture* was that nowhere in this writing was there the ethic of care that Patricia Hill Collins had so powerfully placed at the very heart of her call to action. What would an anthropology that took this seriously look like? What would it feel like?

BEYOND
ESTRANGEMENT

'Epistemology is (not) a bloodless abstraction; the way we know has powerful implications for the way we live. . . every epistemology tends to become an ethic, and every way of knowing tends to become a way of living.' Parker Palmer

Before I knew it, anthropology's way of knowing had become my way of living. It brought with it an odd contradiction. At the same time as anthropology invites you to get close to people to be able to participate, it also requires you to remain distant enough to observe. Together, they make for an odd combination. Becoming familiar with people and then estranging yourself in order to pay close attention call on different qualities in us as humans.

I've come to think of the work of the anthropologist as consisting of three stages. The first is making the strange familiar. You spend the first weeks or months in a state of curiosity about everything that is different, avidly watching, listening, and noticing what's going on around you. You don't quite know at that stage what's important, so you're just gathering up little fragments of information and storing them for later when they may or may not be important.

You know you've entered the second phase when you start spotting patterns; things fall into place, and you start grasping what is going on. It's a bit like learning a language. You learn a collection of words and verbs. But when people are speaking around you, you miss most of what's going on. Then, gradually, you latch onto the words you recognise. Piecing them together gives you the gist of what people are saying.

As you get better at filling in the blanks, you begin to notice words that appear repeatedly. You get curious about them, look them up or ask people what they mean. With those additional pieces, you then start figuring out whole sentences. Quickly, you begin accumulating words that you haven't heard before and making a stab at what they might mean by the place they have in sentences with words you know.

It's a similar process with finding out about another culture. That first phase of everything seeming a bit strange and different is when you realise that even when you don't think you've been making assumptions, you have. Differences may be quite small, barely perceptible. But close attention brings them into view. This begins to give you some clues as to why people do the things they do in that cultural context. You need to be careful not to read your own assumptions into what people do and to keep your mind open, ask questions, compare when you witness similar behaviour, and test out your insights on people familiar with the culture to see if they make sense.

In that phase, you begin to take instances and turn them into identifiable examples of social phenomena. You come to see patterns in the way people do things, and around you, as that pattern is repeated a few times, you watch as it gathers solidity and takes shape as something that might be one of those unwritten cultural rules that the anthropologist is supposed to be expert in noting, decoding, and recording.

The rite of passage of fieldwork doesn't come only with making sense of what's strange that's at the heart of the second phase of the anthropologist's quest for understanding. It's a part of it, but it's akin to moving to a different country and finding your way around, then getting so used to the place there's nothing much that's strange about it anymore. But there's more to what an anthropologist does than this.

What I've come to see as the third – and defining - stage of the anthropologist's process is what happens when you come back from fieldwork and find yourself in moments when what was once familiar feels strange. It's at that instant that you recognise elements of your own culture that you haven't seen quite as clearly before and start bringing them into question, seeing them through a new lens. From there, you can see patterns that are thrown into sharp relief by the comparisons you're able to bring to them from being immersed in another culture.

It's these reflections on the things that you've taken for granted in your own culture that enable you to deepen the process of sense-making about other cultures. That process of estrangement that accompanies each of these phases is what makes the anthropologist's experience different to that of a traveller, or to just about any other kind of researcher. And, or at least that's the way I came to understand it. It's *this* that makes you an anthropologist.

For all that I could find myself getting lost in philosophical ruminations about the nature of anthropology, I had a more basic problem to resolve. An *epistemological* problem, one concerning the nature of knowledge, and in particular, the status of what I was learning as I layered together the things I heard, observed and found out about in answers to my questions.

I'd started worrying that there were things happening in the general mill of life around me that I was missing because they didn't shout out for my attention and didn't make it into my fieldnotes. I put this down to the fact that I was the one doing the participant observing and of course people were going to say certain things to the white woman in the flowery dress. I'd begun to struggle with the thought that much of what I'd thought I'd learnt was gleaned in chance encounters that could just as easily not have happened. My fieldnotes were full of stories that came from moments when I just happened to be somewhere, to which I was able to bear witness. What might someone else have found out in my place if they'd been there and doing anthropological research *the right way*?

A sense of FOMO - Fear Of Missing Out - gripped me. What else might be happening that I was missing because I wasn't asking the right questions, or people were sparing with their answers? How was I going to know what else was going on in Ilemi? It was a variation on the moment of sonder I'd experienced in

Stanley as we drove in the rain to Ibadan; that recognition of co-existence, of a larger picture with myriad individual stories with which mine was entwined in ways I couldn't even begin to appreciate.

When I wrote my ethnography, I wanted to feel it was grounded in something solid. That I'd done my research. But so far all I had was those neatly labelled blue-carbon record books in which I'd diligently recorded the day's events and conversations. I'd barely done any formal interviews. Even when I had, I'd had a distinct feeling that the answers to my questions were given to provide the anthropologist with what they'd like to hear. In fact, it had put me off conventional semi-structured interviewing as a method. It felt too starchy, too pre-planned and disjointed.

What I liked most was the flowing conversation that could take twists and turns, yielding unexpected truths and a certain intimacy that came in the listening. But how rigorous was this? How much of it was people telling me things because I was me?

It got me ruminating again. Surely the knowledge that the anthropologist produces is an artefact of their experience. Others may visit the same place and have an entirely different experience. This is not to say that there aren't things that I can describe about the Nigeria I encountered that you wouldn't also find it you went there too. But there's also something of the self that I brought to those encounters and what I made of them.

If I'd been a different kind of person, would I have so readily taken up the invitation extended to me to stay the night with strangers in a town that I was just passing through? If I'd found myself a different assistant, I'd have had access to entirely different social networks. If I had not gone for a Mrs Mainstream persona, but presented myself exactly as I am, how different would my conversations have been? How much of what I was being told a version for the *oyinbo*? How much was it down to the relationships I made, the other things that people saw and heard of me as I moved around the town, subject wherever I went to curiosity that was a match for mine?

I'd always been critical of the ways in which people who gathered quantitative data presented it as superior to the way in which anthropologists worked, with their fieldnotes and headnotes, impressions and hunches. As if we were lesser to them, lacking in rigour and substance. It irritated the hell out of me. I'd seen for myself how a badly phrased question could bring in completely misleading answers, which then got counted and treated as some kind of truth because there were numbers involved.

I started hankering for the comforts of a methodology that could give me some sense of certainty that I was on the right track.

I decided to do the unthinkable. A survey.

I'd set the questions in advance. Stick to them. Same questions for everyone. One by one, in the same order every time. I knew I couldn't do it myself; I was rubbish at sticking to the script and quickly got distracted into people's stories. I'd find someone else to apply it. I could then treat what it yielded with appropriate distance.

It would allow me to do some finding out that might otherwise be harder to do.

THE SURVEY

Once I'd decided to do the survey, I busied myself with practicalities. I'd need to get it translated into Yoruba and what came back from it into English. This presented me with a challenge. Those acts of translation would be critical. How a question is put so often frames how people answer it. Ask a question a different way and you might get quite a different answer.

This, I reflected, was why I've never trusted surveys. There's too much going on in the encounter between an enumerator asking those questions and the people they're asking that goes unrecorded in analysing survey returns. Let alone the tales of enumerators sitting under trees filling in the surveys themselves when they get bored of asking the questions or struggle to find respondents.

But the idea continued to appeal. I liked the idea of making a list of the things I'd like to know about. I also liked the idea of getting someone else to put those questions to people in Ilemi, someone who'd be able to filter out the kinds of things that would be told to a foreigner who was presumed ignorant or suspected to be after something else.

This way I would be able to operate at arm's reach and do what research methodologists call 'triangulation': comparing sources of information to arrive at a sense of whether there was a fit between them, and a sense of assurance that what was being said was corroborated by others. It was comforting to think of someone else asking the same questions of different people and seeing what they came up with.

Before that could happen there was another challenge to overcome. I had to figure out what the survey would be about. Only then would I be able to find the right person to administer it for me. The previous weeks had brought a lot of lines of enquiry. The impact of the sky-rocketing prices of imported goods. The magical medicines used by women and men to punish or catch or charm their lovers. Reproductive ailments. Useless husbands. Smuggler boys and the political economy of contraband. Abortifacients. Varieties of witchcraft. Most of these didn't lend themselves easily to the use of surveys.

I continued undeterred. There's something about choosing a method before figuring out quite how to apply it. It feels like it's the wrong way round. But I knew that only certain kinds of answers can ever be found through an instrument as crude as a survey. I ran through the options, mulling over and then dismissing each one in turn, until I got to one that worked.

I decided to start with the market. I went there every day; it ebbed and flowed with people as the four-day cycle of markets rotated. I reasoned, there were always people to interview as they were sitting in their stalls all day. There was a period in the mid-afternoon when it went so quiet that there were barely any customers. Ideal conditions for a survey. I had a mental image of the enumerator going from stall to stall with one of those clipboards and a sheaf of survey forms, diligently filling in a growing pile of returns. At its busiest, the market must have had a couple of hundred people selling their wares.

I'd already got some numbers from counting the vendors of particular goods, to get a mental map of the market and its demography. It was during the phase in which I was intrigued about what it did for relationships between vendors to be sitting so closely together, vying for the same customers.

I found myself switching on a different bit of my brain.

For weeks and months, I'd been following the stories people told me. My entire sensibility had been geared at openness, at listening and at creating a safe, empathetic, intimacy with the speaker so that they felt they could unburden themselves. Now I had to think in a much more linear and instrumental way. It didn't come easily. But once I got into the spirit of it, I found myself liking the idea that I could arrive at a list of questions that could be asked of absolutely everyone in the same way and that would generate answers that could be compared and even - to give me the kinds of data I was after - *crunched* to deliver some statistics.

In this way, I arrived at the purpose of the survey, which was to map out what was happening as the macro-economic environment changed with the adoption of structural adjustment. It would help me tell the story of change that I was seeing and hearing about around me.

Nigeria was at the time taking a dose of the same medicine that had caused fatal side-effects in economies elsewhere in Africa, a remedy purported as something of an economic cure-all. Those numbers would allow me to put the human beings into the story, in a way that would be legible to those for whom the hard facts of the matter start with tables and tests of significance.

That was the theory. I had some quite basic questions that were ideal for a survey. I wanted to know where those who were selling goods in the market came from. This would give me a picture of the extent to which the market was serving the economic activity of the hamlets that lay around the town and map the participation of traders from within the town and from the ring of market towns that lay at some distance from Ilemi.

I could ask about their trading careers. When they'd begun trading in that particular line of goods. Whether they'd shifted what they did in the face of shortages and price rises, like the switch to home-made soap or the burgeoning market in second-hand clothes. I could ask about their suppliers, and whether they'd had to go further afield as goods became scarcer or more expensive.

I put together a long list of questions, edited them into a shorter checklist and interspersed closed and open questions, with enough in there to be able to quantify the results if I had enough respondents. I thought about how best to create a sample, that is, a way to select those who would answer the survey systematically. I opted for random sampling along a transect crossing the market from one corner to another. This would involve drawing a mental line that cut across the market and stopping at every fifth stall along the way to ask the person questions.

All set.

I wrote out the questions neatly on a sheet of typing paper, folded it twice and put it inside a fresh lined notebook. It all seemed very innocuous.

When Iya Dayo turned up for work the next morning, I presented her with the notebook and instructions to head to the market to begin the survey.

She eyed me sceptically.

"Those market women are not going to want to tell me anything," she said. "They will think I am trying to steal their market or ask for money for their answers as I am surely being paid to ask them."

I brushed off her doubts. "But we've gone around town asking people all kinds of things and no-one has refused so far."

"That," she said, "is because they will talk with you. They don't want to share their secrets with someone who is like them. They will think I am finding all of this out to steal their market or to bring them down, so they fail."

"Let's give it a try?" I pleaded. "I just want you to test it out to see what happens when you ask these questions. Then we can find someone else who will do the survey."

A look of resignation fell over Iya Dayo's face. She took the notebook and put it into her bag, then left for the market without a backwards glance.

An hour later she was back. "Those women! They refused to tell me anything. They said, 'where is our money?'. They said they wanted to be paid for making the video."

"Making the video?"

"They said that these questions are for making a video and they want to be paid before they answer."

Where did the idea of making a video come from, I wondered? Was it that people had come across researchers asking questions before and the next thing they knew, there was someone with a film camera? Or had people watched filming in markets on the news, and assumed the questions were the kind that was asked by reporters? It wouldn't be too long a shot to imagine this, I reasoned, given the amount of news coverage that the economic situation was getting.

Whatever the matter, it was obvious that this was going to be a non-starter.

The survey was quietly abandoned. But what happened when I asked more directly about the impact of economic change on trade was intriguing. If those news cameras had descended on Ilemi's marketwomen, they would have captured eloquent denouncements of the IMF and the World Bank and as articulate an analysis of the shortcomings of their economic policies as I'd heard from the mouths of any commentator.

OF DOGS AND MEN

I wasn't yet done with surveys. I was taken by the principle of someone else asking the same questions to different people and being able to compare and learn from what people told them with what they'd told me. I also thought it would be useful to have a way of assessing more how widespread certain beliefs or practices were in a more systematic way. With all of this, I reasoned, it might still be worth applying a survey.

If ways of making money was too contentious, I'd ask about sex instead.

A few weeks before, after a long day in the local customary court working through their records, I'd decided to hire a research assistant to transcribe cases for me. I was in search of something more systematic than flicking through cases and homing in on the ones that grabbed my attention. The idea was to pull out all the cases that related to marriage, divorce, paternity, custody, and adultery, to look at patterns: incidence, judgements, payments. As with pretty much everything, I didn't quite know at that stage what I would do with what I found. But I was intrigued enough to invest some effort in finding out.

The search for a research assistant landed me a lad who'd just finished school and had time on his hands. Son of the husband-and-wife team who ran one of the many churches in town, Paul had grown up in the town. He knew lots of young men. I was interested in their side of the refrain that I was constantly hearing, including from young people themselves, that the young women of today were out of control, *uselessing themselves all around* and *running here and there after men.*

Presumably, I thought to myself, young men were part of all of this - although no-one seemed to quite put it that way. In fact, I'd rarely heard any of the narrative cast aspersion on *men's* behaviour. That is, apart from the *fayawo* boys and that was more geared to the easy come, easy go lucre associated with smuggling. Even then, the main focus of disapproval was the women who those smuggler boys would charm with their cash.

Here, I thought, was a good opportunity to apply a survey. I'd come up with a list of questions. I'd then send Paul to interview his friends and associates around the town. I wasn't going to design it in as formal a way as the survey that had failed. At this stage, it was just exploratory. A kind of pre-test. It would help me see what could be discovered if I sent someone else out to ask the kind of questions that would be difficult for me to ask myself. I went through the things that I was interested in finding out. I homed in on a set of topics. They reflected my growing concern with the risks young people might be taking - with HIV, fertility-limiting sexually transmitted diseases and unsafe abortion.

I sent Paul off with an orange cover ruled notebook that I'd bought for him to record responses to the questions.

A couple of days later he bounced into the basement. I was dipping lumps of *eba* into a plateful of stew and chatting to Grace. He looked very pleased with himself.

"How did it go?" I asked.

"Very interesting!" he said. "Very".

I had my hands full and gestured to him to leave the book on the table. There was something unsaid, a trace of a smirk playing on his lips.

"Thank you! Come back tomorrow, Paul. I'll read this tonight and we can then discuss."

He eyed me with a look that I could only describe as mischievous, and then he was off, up the steps.

I wondered what was in the notebook.

I went to wash my hands, then took the book to my perch on the roof to settle down to read, grabbing my cigarettes on the way. I almost choked when I read the first page. Then I burst out laughing. What I held in my hands was a survey of sexual positions, in answer to a rather badly put question about what kind of sex is risky for HIV transmission.

Doggy position, it turned out.

SCHOOL FOR LIFE

What I read in the pages of Paul's orange notebook intrigued me. It was a window into the world of the adolescents I'd taught. The stories they'd written for their English assignments when I was teaching at St Botolph's began to take on a new meaning. I was curious to find out more.

I didn't think I could send Paul back to ask more questions, and it might well prove tricky to find a young woman his age to talk to others like her. This is where the anthropologist comes unstuck: quite obviously, I couldn't don a cloak of invisibility and hang out with young women. Nor were they likely to chat to me, given that I'd so recently been a teacher. My indeterminate age and my whiteness counted against me getting anywhere at all.

This, I thought, is where doing a survey would come into its own. But not the kind of survey I'd sent Iya Dayo to the market to try out. Or the checklist I'd despatched with Paul. The best way to find out the answers to those questions, I reckoned, was to administer a questionnaire that people fill in for themselves. Anonymously.

I hit on an idea. I'd ask the head teacher in each of the town's secondary schools to allow me to administer the questionnaire in a study period. The young people would be a captive audience. I'd hand out the questionnaires and some nice pens that they could keep as a thank you. I'd explain what the questionnaire was going to be used for. Ask them if they'd be willing to fill it in as truthfully as possible. Tell them they didn't need to put their names on the forms. Assure them that no-one would know the answers were theirs, as I was going to ask them to bring the questionnaires to the front of the class and put them in a heap, all mixed up. It would be a bit like administering an exam. Time up and I'd collect the scripts.

It took some while to design the survey. I put together an initial list of possible ways of asking and used one of my trips to Ibadan to test them out on some university students I met at a student canteen on campus. They helped me reframe them and come up with some more questions that might be asked. I then borrowed a typewriter, typed the questionnaire out neatly and took it to the photocopy shop, where it was all nicely copied and stapled.

I felt very pleased with myself. This had all the makings of a proper, systematic, approach that could generate the kind of reliable data I'd come to crave.

Back in Ilemi, I put the plan into action. Within a day, I had 100 questionnaire returns in my hands. Third time lucky. The truths told on those pages gave me a window into a world that I could otherwise not have found my way into. And they took me in a direction that brought me back to the place where I began. Almost a third of the young women and almost the same number of young men reported using ways of 'bringing down a pregnancy' – using as abortifacients handfuls of pills, cupfuls of washing powder, worse. There was widespread ignorance about HIV. Many of the girls had experienced unpleasant discharges.

It was a sexual health timebomb. The question was, what could I do about it?

Anthropologists don't often trouble themselves about what their fieldwork is *for*. It's considered enough that they'd produce articles, a monograph, give papers at conferences, contribute Knowledge. But what if you your data starts telling you that people are going to suffer or die if things carry on the way they are? My training taught me that the role of the anthropologist was to document culture rather than try to change people's behaviour. It had instilled in me the moral principle of *do no harm*. There was little sense in that training that the anthropologist might also have a moral obligation to do what they could to *prevent* harm or indeed to *do good*.

Anthropological ethics included making sure that no harm came from the research activities of the anthropologist. It included things like making sure that people's identities were protected in the accounts that were later written about them. It also included taking care that confidentiality was kept so that what people shared of their lives would not be identified directly with them, especially if it could in any way cause them to be placed in danger. But there wasn't really any discussion in my anthropology classes about what to do if you came across practices and beliefs that were harmful during your fieldwork. I think the expectation was that you'd do as with any other aspect of the culture: write it down in your fieldnotes, then write it up in your thesis.

Applied anthropology was for professionals. At this stage, I was just a student. What could I do that would have any meaning, anyway? I'd been troubled by the idea that as an anthropology student I could just take myself to whatever corner of the globe I found interesting to study. If that wasn't bad enough, what about feeling myself entitled to start interfering in people's lives once I got there? Wasn't that indefensibly colonial? What right did I have to stray beyond being a visitor and a guest into actively trying to intervene in the community that had so kindly taken me in and made me feel so loved? Surely, though, if that love was reciprocal, didn't I then have a moral duty to do what I could in the face of the disaster that loomed?

These are the kinds of questions that might propel someone from anthropology towards medicine, international development, engineering or to a pursuit that feels more useful. That's the effect that doing anthropology ultimately had on me.

I couldn't sustain doing nothing more than observe and record. Nor was I capable of the kind of conservatism that I came to associate with the idea that the anthropologist was simply there to document life with as much objectivity as possible. I wanted to be part of making change happen. I wanted to be able to do something if I encountered harms, not just do no harm.

Many anthropologists regard acting on this kind of impulse like stepping over an invisible line. Once you're over, you're gone. I remember the story told by one of my professors of a terrible drought in the place where he was doing his fieldwork. All around him, people were getting sick and dying. He had a Land Rover. He could have used it to take people to hospital. But he decided that this was not what he was there for. Instead, he focused on his fieldwork. Later he published a book that made no mention of the drought, or the struggles of the people he lived amongst for survival during those times. It told, in what's called the 'ethnographic present' – a device that makes the account of the anthropologist timeless - of rites and rituals.

I shared these thoughts with Margaret. She brought me sharply back down to earth. A few weeks earlier, we'd gone together to the British Consulate in Lagos, where I'd witnessed at first hand the indignities that people applying for visas to the UK were put through. Her docket of papers included the wrist band given to her daughter at birth, a thick wad of bank statements, letters from her daughter, photographs of the family. The visa service had been unresponsive to her pointing out to them that she'd been visiting Britain for more than twenty years. Why would she stay when she had an entire life, a business, family, and friends, to return to?

"And why," she muttered to me as we sat waiting for the appointment she'd finally got, "would they think would I want to live in that country anyway?"

I'd protested that there wasn't really anything much I could do if I came with her, a white person to add to the bundle of statements, photos, and memories. But in the event, the very whiteness of my presence secured us the kind of result Margaret had hoped it would achieve.

Margaret didn't mince her words. A widow of a successful local man, she was one of those women who people would describe as being able to 'do and undo'. She'd won the respect of the town's modernisers, her years in the UK, her connections with big men beyond the town and her status as the proprietor of the town's largest hotel lending her gravitas.

Now I was sitting in the lounge of her hotel, sharing my dilemmas. The fan was whirring, the gusts of cooling air a welcome relief in the cloying heat of the late afternoon. The first mosquitoes of the evening had ventured out and were busy helping themselves to my ankles. A cold beer sat in front of me.

She folded her arms as she listened.

I began to feel embarrassed just looking at the expression on her face.

"So, what is it that are you proposing that you can do?"

I mumbled something about health promotion activities. Posters. Leaflets. Talks. Working with schools and clinics. Raising awareness. Running workshops. Getting some funding to do this from a development agency.

Margaret drew the line at this. As I'd already become more than aware, she had no time at all for international development agencies.

It was, in her view, a white person's folly.

"This development is just about developing richer countries. It does nothing for us. Look at what those people are doing to this country!", she proclaimed.

"Focus on your studies, get a decent job, then you can have children. Don't waste your time with this nonsense."

THE CHIEF, THE DRIVER AND HIS MISTRESS

"Anna, you go give me jedi-jedi o!" Dapo complained, groaning loudly.

He turned to grin at me. I'd been installed in what was known as the owner's seat – directly behind him - and was offering him another piece of homemade stewed pineapple. I had protested at the seating arrangements; it felt like being the Madam. I'd had to work hard enough on getting Dapo to call me "Anna" rather than "Miss Anna", a name that conjured up an image in my mind of a severe-looking governess with a starched white collar from some book I'd read as a child.

Grace and Margaret had found Dapo for me, insisting that it was unsafe to persist in driving Stanley myself on long distance journeys – especially on my own and especially around Lagos. And that's where we were going today.

Homesickness manifests in many strange forms. For me, it was all about food. The food of my childhood, some of which I had never particularly liked. I'd woken up that morning with the taste of one of those foods in my mouth: syrupy tinned pineapple chunks that were served for school dinners with vanilla ice cream, topped with a glace cherry. I'd procured a pineapple, running to the market in my jeans, to the hoots and laughter of the market women who had only ever seen me in a *buba* and wrapper. I'd chopped it into slices, then into the triangular chunks of the tinned variety that was occupying my thoughts. I then boiled it with a liberal quantity of sugar to make the syrup.

I was decidedly proud of my confection. Proud enough to bring it on the trip to Lagos.

Dapo's lithe lean-limbed body was clothed in dust-caked jeans and a tight over-washed T-shirt. Eyeing him in the mirror, I recalled the rumour I'd heard about him some days before that he'd become the lover of a big madam who lived in a newly built concrete house with a grandiose portico. The woman was one of those wives who demanded nothing less than the finest lace and was only to be seen behind the misted window of her husband's Mercedes, never dirtying her jewelled sandals with the dust of Ilemi's mud paths. Her husband was, or so people said, an Alhaji with business interests in Lagos. He was often away. The way the story was told, his absence was an invitation, as well as an explanation. Small wonder that small town boy Dapo had become more than her driver.

'Outside wives' were a menace that women whose husbands had a bit of money had to brace themselves to expect, so that when it happened it wasn't the kind of wrenching surprise that turns your world upside down. They'd said to me, *our men are like that, men are like that, that's what men are like, that's what our Nigerian men are like.*

But for a woman of means to have a lithe lean-limbed young man tending to her needs was positively scandalous. For all that it was frowned upon, theirs was more of an open secret than a secret affair. I mean, even I knew about it. It had all the makings of the lurid tales that crowded the pages of *Intimate Affairs*, *Hints* and the Nigerian equivalent of the National Inquirer, *Lagos*

Weekend.

I'd begun a small collection of those magazines, hoarding them in a big iron box under my bed, in case they'd yield me the topic for my PhD. Their headlines were fabulous. There was a sprinkling of the magical and the absurd. Lagos Weekend had recently carried a story headlined *"Nurse Revives Dead Organ"*. It spoke to a malady sweeping through the motor parks of the region believed to be caused by men shaking hands with mystery carriers of the 'virus' and finding themselves impotent. Men would present at the clinic as the victims and, or so claimed the article, find themselves revived in the hands of a nurse.

Well-known international news stories found a Nigerian twist in these pages. My favourite was *"Lorena Bobbitt, I've been there too"*, retelling the apocryphal tale of the American woman who chopped off her violent husband's penis and threw it out of the window of a car, only to let her remorse wash over her enough to go back to retrieve it. Mr Bobbitt had it sewed back on and went on to become a minor porn star.

This was a time when another virus, HIV, was stalking the land, invisible to us all. Ignoring Margaret's caution about intervening, I'd decided that the least I could do was raise awareness and do whatever I could to encourage people to protect themselves from infection. I'd gone to Planned Parenthood in Lagos, explaining my dilemma and asking for their help. They gave me access to as many boxes of free condoms as I could carry. I'd taken to bringing boxes of condoms back from Lagos with me along with the brown bags full of bundles of Naira notes.

Dapo, Remi and a handful of other lads helped distribute them. They'd come to my room in the twilight hours and fill their pockets with the little metal packets; I'd hoped that they made use of them. But for Dapo, my HIV prevention efforts came too late. The Alhaji had, no doubt, spun his own skein of risky encounters. Dapo's was the first death I mourned when I returned to the UK.

The lads were part of my ambitious plans for persuading the young men of Ilemi into using condoms. But Mrs Mainstream wasn't helping. I realized that the identity I'd slid so comfortably into was really getting in the way. It was one thing to cruise through a police checkpoint. It was another to convince people that Mrs Mainstream was not going to judge them if they told me the inconvenient truths about love, money, and everyday life that my research was turning out to be about.

I concluded that as Mrs Mainstream, no-one was going to tell me anything interesting at all. What was I to do? I'd worked so hard at being proper, at gaining the kind of respectability that was so much a hallmark of pride amongst my older friends in the town and of which my mother would have approved, along with the flowery dresses. And in all that time, it hadn't really occurred to me that the identity I had been so busy constructing wasn't going to do me any favours when it came to finding out what was *really* going on.

One day I came back with a white polystyrene dildo from a trip to Lagos to change money and stock up on boxes of condoms. Within minutes of spotting a large pile of dildos on the table in the Planned Parenthood office, I had one in my hands.

The polystyrene dildo liberated me.

I became bold and then brazen. "Sorry-o!" women would chorus, roaring with raucous laughter, when I whipped it out to demonstrate how to put on a condom. They'd heard, they told me, about the fact that white men were not very well endowed. The little white penis said it all.

I took to using large empty Guinness bottles, rolling condoms over their improbable girth. We'd fall about with giggles, like teenagers.

Those hoots that I'd been greeted with when I ran into the market to buy pineapple wearing my jeans, I realised, told me that for all those flowery dresses and Grace's tailor's attempts to recreate designer fashions with the bales of local cloth I'd hauled back from Abeokuta's cloth market, I could have been wearing jeans all along. It might have led me to some very different stories.

That's the thing about being an anthropologist. It's not only who you talk with. It's how those who you talk with see you and, I came to think, how they might imagine being received by you – whether you'd judge them, or find them strange or funny, or spill or keep their secrets. Stands to reason, really. Just that, along with most of the other things I'd come to experience in my fieldwork, it wasn't really talked about in my anthropology classes.

I didn't take to wearing jeans. It was too hot. But I did come down from my perch on the roof above the motor park and smoke my cigarettes and drink my beer in the town's bars. There I met women like the one from Lagos who I'd been warned away from. They told me stories of unreliable charmers with get-rich-quick money that would be there one minute and gone the next, of husbands who accumulated women and deposited them in homes all over town. Their stories of love and money were like something out of *Hints* or *Intimate Affairs*. And in retelling them, they were bold, frank and often hilarious.

Here, I thought, were examples of the women's empowerment that had so intrigued me and brought me to Nigeria in the first place. They wouldn't be seen as such by the stout guardians of the town's morality, the kind of women who became stalwarts of Nigeria's Better Life for Rural Women programme – nicknamed Better Life for *Richer* Women as, like the First Lady herself who'd been the public face of this rural development programme - there was clearly something in it for them. But now I was no longer Mrs Mainstream, I had access to them and could take into my enquiry a much broader seam of everyday life in the town than had been possible before.

Lubricated by beer, the ambiance of low lighting and low-slung sofa seats, men of all generations would strike up a conversation. They'd talk to me as if to a confidante. Rarely would anyone come on to me. Nor did my presence seem to be experienced as shocking or anomalous. I became in my whiteness someone whose gender was ambiguous, what anthropologists might term an 'honorary male'.

Those men would tell me the saddest of stories, tales of love and loss, of broken hearts and betrayal. They'd talk about their love for their children and their mothers, and of frictions at home with wives pitted against sisters and accusations flying of *juju* and witchcraft and envy and spite. And sometimes, they'd tell me their life stories; the excitement of migrating to work in Lagos, which had drawn generations of young people from the town like a magnet, falling in love, troubles with their marriages, managing misfortune, staying alive.

I'd left behind Mrs Mainstream, all proper and prim. I finally felt as if I was able to be myself. I began to see the town through different eyes. And seeing me in different places, the town began to relate to me differently too. One night, I organised a screening of HIV prevention films in the town hall. I accompanied it with one of my now-deft condom demos. I'd begin by pulling the polystyrene dildo out of my bag and then, to howls of laughter, replace it with one of those large beer bottles, which I'd proceed to encase in one of the condoms. It had a touch of stand-up comedy to it. I'd end up doing the banter, then dissolving into laughter with the crowd.

After people had dissipated and I wandered back along the road, I was called over by a couple of young men. We stood in the road for half an hour or more, chatting. About the kind of women who people called 'eat and run'. About relationships, pleasures, desires, taboos, injunctions, norms, fears. About oral sex, and whether it could give you HIV. About itches, discharges, chills, boils, and all manner of bodily detail of the kind that it would take a doctor to want to enquire too deeply about.

I felt as if what I was finding out had moved to a different level of depth. I'd spent months roving around the town with my questions. Being left directionless by my abandoned project had given me an unexpected freedom to pursue anything that piqued my interest. For a generation of anthropologists who grew of age in a discipline gripped by angst about positionality and relevance, having to reinvent my project from scratch liberated me in unexpected ways. I could do little else but explore alternatives, as there was no obvious route to follow.

My meanderings led me down blind alleys, into cul-de-sacs, into the Nigerian equivalent of stately homes and council estates, always curious about the people I encountered and their everyday lives. Where, ultimately, it led me was back to where I began my journey with anthropology: a quest to understand what it means to be human.

A DAY OUT AT
THE SEASIDE

Carburettor smooth as silk and with only the slightest judder in his movements, Stanley felt reborn. I'd lingered for as long as I could in the mechanics' yard, half an eye trained on Remi and his boys as they forayed into Stanley's bowels, while his boss Henri wore my ears out with a stream of consciousness that drifted promiscuously between Baudelaire and the current state of politics in Benin. My French was progressing nicely, but not quite nicely enough to engage in this kind of chat.

The sun seemed to burn hotter than ever. Almost a week's electricity outage ensured that there was no salvation to be found in a cold Coca Cola. The desire to immerse myself in cold water overwhelmed me. A fantasy slowly formed in my mind, then rolled like a gentle wave over my entire body. Badagry Beach was only an hour or so's drive away. I'd gather the kids and whoever else fancied going, and off we'd go to the seaside.

An hour later, Stanley was ready.

An excited gaggle of children piled into the back of the car. I counted. There were fourteen of us. Stanley's burgundy velour seats were capacious enough for four in the front. I shared mine with one of the children, my leg crammed next to the gear shaft. In the back, piled on top of each other were another eight people, the adults anchoring layers of children who laughed, and squirmed, and screamed with joy. When I protested that this was all totally illegal, they told me to stop being so English. I started the engine and we lurched forward.

Once we got going, Stanley cruised amiably along with his precious cargo. Half-way towards Badagry we hit a police roadblock. I'd come to regard the local police as relatively benign after my visit to the police station to commission one of the constables to draw me a map of the town.

It was Baba Tinu's idea. "These people know the town," he'd said, "you can't trust them for anything else, but they'll know their beats. Offer them N100 and they will do anything you ask of them."

And indeed, so they did. I was summoned back to pick up the map, a big piece of blue card beautifully coloured in, the contours of the main roads and settlements clearly marked. There had been an unexpected benefit: jovial exchanges whenever I ventured out of town. Sometimes they would pull me over, but only to exchange pleasantries. Most of the time, they just shouted a greeting and waved me on.

Today was, however, a rather different scenario. I was driving a car with fourteen people in it, blatantly breaking the law. I drew Stanley to a crawling speed as we approached the check point. My mind spun with possible excuses, drawing blanks. My heart began pounding. The last thing I needed right now was to have my car impounded again. My passengers hadn't picked up on my nervous silence and the car felt fuller still with their noisy excitement and peals of laughter. I felt like saying "shhhh..." but realised it would be utterly futile. All the police had to do was to slow us down and peer into my window to see Tade squished up against the gear shaft, and Ayomide balancing on Iya Bola's knees next to me.

"Don't be so English!" I admonished myself.

But I *was* English. That was the problem. I wouldn't exactly slip by with this infraction. I hadn't learnt how to bribe properly. I hadn't even learnt how to beg my way out of situations like this properly.

We inched forward. There were four policemen. Three sat in a makeshift check point by the side of the road, and I could see the fourth flagging down the vehicle in front of me. Maybe we could slip by while he was distracted. But he quickly waved the vehicle on. He turned to face us as we drew closer. And then I recognised his face. It was the constable who had drawn the map. Beaming.

"Miss Anna!" he said, with delight.

"Ẹ ku ojo meta!" I called back with an affectionate greeting that you'd give to someone you hadn't seen for a while.

"Se alaafia ni?" I loved the word a*laafia*. It was one of those untranslatable ones, a concept that rolled together feeling good in mind, spirit, and body.

"*Adupe-o*," he shouted, waving us on with a cheerful smile.

An uneventful hour or so later, we arrived at Badagry beach. The children spilled out of the car, whooping with excitement, and we gathered ourselves up and walked through the fringe of palm trees to greet the expanse of the ocean.

Waves roared and crashed onto the sand, spitting gallons of foam, and dragging the shore with them as they washed away. I grabbed the hands of two of the children. We ran into the ocean, screaming with joy, jumping through the waves, and laughing. They ran back to the rest of the group, and I stood there alone, waves crashing against my calves, looking out to sea.

It was not far from this beach to the whitewashed buildings with their cannons and dungeons from which so many thousands were trafficked into slavery. Those who got as far as this place on the edge of the ocean were the strongest and fittest. Many more died as they were marched, shackled together, to the slave ports, and in dank, dark holding places that were called 'factories'. An estimated two million slaves died on what was called 'the Middle Passage' – the second leg of the triangular trading route that ran from Britain to West Africa, from West Africa to the Americas, and from there back to Britain. Those who survived found new horrors awaiting them at the other side, sold into chattel slavery, beaten, raped, starved, and abused. Those who could not be sold were slaughtered like animals.

As I gazed out at the landless horizon, I thought about the role the British had played in commercialising the capture and sale of human beings. Was the Atlantic slave trade made possible by the same mindset that classified people into categories of humans rather than as part of a shared human race, making them less deserving of humanity? Or was it just greed? In *Das Capital*, Marx wrote that "... the turning of Africa into a warren for the commercial hunting of black-skins signalled the rosy dawn of the era of capitalist production". For Marx, the slave trade was an example of what he called 'primitive accumulation' of capital, which preceded and made possible the industrialisation of Britain. That certainly wasn't something that we were taught in History lessons at school.

I knew this much: The British brought guns, booze, and trinkets to trade. Human life was cheap. An umbrella for a king or a chief cost ten people, the same for a bottle of spirits. Slaves provided the labour that supplied the sweetness of the drink that was introduced to Britain as the British Empire came into its ascendant and became synonymous with Britishness in the colonial era: tea. British industrialists used tea to extract longer hours from their workers.

In this way, the wealth made through sugar and slavery fuelled the industrial revolution in Britain. But industrialisation also hastened its end. Machines needed lubricants. Mass production of foodstuffs and cosmetics required a cheap form of oil. The "Slave Coast" was home to a species of palm tree that had been used for generations in cooking, to make soap and other cosmetics, as a salve for medicaments, as roofing and weaving material, and for a host of other uses. Palm oil became 'red gold' in the period in which the British sought to shift the international slave trade to what they called 'the legitimate trade'. In the words of historian Martin Lynn, palm oil literally "grease[d] the wheels of the industrial revolution".[6]

I knew some other things: Palm oil production and trade was women's work. It was arduous, messy work to pound the palm fruit to extract rich red oil, and roast and crack the shells of the palm nuts to release the oil-rich kernels. Early in my time in Ilemi, I'd wandered down to the river and watched as women stamped on vats of palm fruit to pound the oil out. Small palm oil-processing stalls lined the river and were supplied by canoe with fruits harvested by young men and brought in jute sackfuls. Kernel cracking machines whirred and crunched nuts that had been hand-cleaned by women in big basins of water. Big jerrycans of rich red palm oil used for dishes like my favourite *egusi* soup were head loaded to market every four days, for sale by the bottleful for domestic use.

I also knew that in the past, as well as the present, women traders worked on their own account; their husbands were supposed to give them starting capital on marriage, but any profits were theirs to keep, and it had been this way for generations. I'd been told a tale of a past, *n'igba atijo* - the golden, olden days - in which women were obedient, chaste, and contained. Older women told me that they'd barely even been allowed to set eyes on the man their parents had chosen for them before the *idana*, where the first tranche of the dowry was paid along with ritual offerings of kola nut. And I'd been treated to a litany of complaints about men not supporting their households, *as if this was what had been expected of them in the past.*

Now, as I looked out at the sea, I began piecing things together. My mind was whirring, making connections between fragments of information that I hadn't seen before. That's also part of the research process. I'd got so caught up in finding out about relationships recently that I'd lost sight of that early period of finding-out that had involved topics as apparently random as the making of palm oil, the wars that were so fierce the people of the town had constructed a wall around it, the names of the different quarters that told where the *alejo* who settled had come to the town from, and the oral histories of marriage and of work.

Suddenly, it all gained a new relevance.

I realised that what I'd come to know about slavery was very patchy. Like most British people, I'd heard the story of William Wilberforce that told of his heroic efforts to end the slave trade and how when he'd won over Parliament, Britain led the world in efforts to close the trade down. I'd also heard inspiring stories of resistance, mutinies, and rebellions amongst the enslaved. I'd learnt of the Toussaint L'Ouverture and how he'd led the slave revolt in Haiti that led to the end of slavery there, and that was to sound a death knell for slavery worldwide. I'd heard songs and legends celebrating Zumbi of Palmares, the king of one of Brazil's most famous *quilombos* - self-governing communities of escaped slaves – that had grown to be the size of Portugal by the time he died in 1695.

Like many other white academics, I'd become fascinated by the religious syncretism and arts of what came to be called 'the Black Atlantic'. Robert Farris Thompson's book *Flash of the Spirit: African and Afro-American Art and Philosophy* coined the term to describe the cultural imprint of the religion, cuisine, and culture of five West African cultures, including Yoruba. Paul Gilroy embodied it in his landmark book of that title, defining it as 'the polyphonic qualities of black cultural expression'.[7]

In Salvador, the Brazilian city where over 80% of people are of African descent and just 3% of the slaves arriving there in the early 19th century were *not* Yoruba, I'd met the inspiring French anthropologist and photographer Pierre Fátúmbí Verger. He'd photographed and written about and become himself a devotee of the *orisa*, the religion brought by the Yoruba. He'd also documented the sheer scale of the traffic.[8]

An estimated one in five of the 17m people stolen from Africa in the slave trade were Yoruba. That was one hell of a lot of people. And those were the ones who survived.

There's been estimates of Africa losing between 30m and 100m people as a result of the slave trade - deaths in the wars that were fought as well as the raids to supply the trade, in the caravans that brought them to the coast, from raging disease and appalling conditions as they waited to be transported, from disease or malnutrition or being thrown to sea once on board, in waves of illness that swept through the 'seasoning camps' where they'd be sequestered on arrival or disposed of when buyers could not be found.

The sheer scale of it all, the monstrousness, the suffering, the inhumanity. It was barely imaginable.

But up to that point, I'd paid far less attention to the consequences for those who were left behind. I thought back to Walter Rodney's *How Europe Underdeveloped Africa*. Its hard-hitting analysis highlighted the economic effects of the slowing of population growth caused by the rupture of wars, slaving raids and the depletion of the continent's strongest and fittest people, over more than five generations. UNESCO's Slave Routes project estimates that Africa's population would have been as much as double in the mid-19th century if there had been no slave trade.[9]

There were more facts to digest. Up to 70% of those who boarded the slave ships were men. What, I wondered, happened to the women who were left behind? And when the British started promoting the 'legitimate trade' and the demand for palm oil soared, when imported goods started flowing into the markets of the interior, what then? What impact had all of this had on women's lives and choices, and on their relationships with men?

It felt as if there was an important missing piece here that I wasn't going to get to by talking to people. I needed to go back to the archives and rummage in the library. I could only understand the present if I got a much better handle on the past.

But first, I needed to get the kids home. We bumped and laughed and sang all the way home and then had a delicious plate of fresh river fish in hot pepper sauce and big sticky pats of *eba* for tea. I went to bed brimming with anticipation of all the finding out I'd need to do.

What I hadn't quite taken on board at that stage was what that would involve.

THE ETHNOGRAPHIC PAST

Anthropologists have something called the 'ethnographic present'. It's a tense that hides history. It also conveniently masks the changes that might have been taking place in the long years that anthropologists spend 'writing up'. Historians and anthropologists share much in common. But amongst anthropologists there can be a carelessness about time past, a tendency to freeze customs and rituals as if they existed out of time, and, at times, what might appear to historians as a cavalier sweep of generalisation about the past. "I envy you being an anthropologist," a historian once said to me by way of a back-handed compliment, "you don't worry so much about evidence."

It was evidence that I was now craving. A different kind of evidence to the footnotes in the history books written largely by white scholars. Some of it might be found in the records painstakingly kept by the colonial authorities, although these were so saturated with their administrative concerns, I'd found barely a trace of information up to that point about the kinds of issues my research was surfacing. I had some notes from observations by the Christian missionaries about women and morality. They confirmed my every prejudice.

I realised that I'd been reading these records for little nuggets of information about the people whose minds they were seeking to colonise, but not paying close enough attention to what they were *saying* about what the missionaries were *doing*.

That's the thing about a piece of historical evidence, or really anything that you read, see, or listen to as a researcher. You take from it what you're looking for, and you can miss loads of things hiding there in plain sight just because you've not currently got them in your sights. You see what you're attuned to notice. You can go back to the same source with different questions and find a whole new story sitting there, waiting to be found.

So that's where I began. I went back to those sources and re-read them. I started piecing together a much more detailed account of what had been going on in the nineteenth century. And with all this, I disappeared down a rabbit hole. What I learned in the process was how much I didn't know.

I realised I didn't really understand that much about how colonialism had actually taken root. I hadn't really thought of it in terms of different phases, with different administrators and the complex mesh of relationships, bargains and motivations that had come with all of that. Or about the big picture – the global economy, the political alliances and economic impact of the two World Wars, or indeed the geopolitical backdrop in terms of international relations between Britain and the other world powers. Or about what Britain was doing there at all.

It sounds naïve, but I'd treated colonialism as a kind of fact, a bad thing that had happened to Nigeria. I was, after all, an anthropologist and we tend to deal with the consequences rather than the causes of things, in the ethnographic present.

In my forays into the past, I'd been far more drawn to finding out about anti-colonial resistance than about how colonisation had taken place. I'd trudged my way through the journals and letters of Anna Hinderer, wife of the Church Missionary Society missionary David Hinderer, brought together in *Seventeen Years in the Yoruba Country: Memorials of Anna Hinderer, Wife of the Rev. David Hinderer C.M.S. Missionary in Western Africa.*[10] It was not a gripping read. I'd looked at the impressions recorded by adventurers like Hugh Clapperton and Richard Lander, and colonial anthropologists.[11] A source as dense and long as the Bible became my go-to account of how things were in the past: the Sierra-Leone born Anglican minister Samuel Johnson's magisterial *History of the Yorubas*.[12] But for all of that reading, I didn't really have the handle on the past that I needed to get to grips with the present.

I went back again to the historical record, with a different agenda. I wanted to understand this history as one in which I was implicated as a white British person.

My working-class white English family had worked for generations in factories in Birmingham, a city that grew out of the industrial revolution. My father's aunt and her entire family worked in Cadbury's chocolate factory. As a child I used to look forward to her parcels of misshapen chocolates. I once ate 24 Cadbury's Crème Egg rejects in one sitting. (And no, I didn't puke). Nigerian cocoa supplied that factory in the colonial era, and palm oil from the 'Slave Coast' lubricated the manufacturing boom that made Birmingham "the city of a thousand trades".[13]

I was born a couple of years after Nigeria won her independence. The post-war British welfare state and the Anglican church created the conditions of possibility for my Brummie working class choirboy father to go to Cambridge university in the mid-1950s, and then for me to study at Oxford in the early 1980s. Margaret Thatcher and Tony Blair hadn't yet conspired to marketise our universities. Escaping the estrangement of rubbing shoulders with the elite, I'd found myself at London University's School of Oriental and African Studies with no less elite a staff and student body, for all that SOAS has come to garner a reputation for being left-wing and anti-establishment. I found out that the School was established in 1916 to train colonial merchants, soldiers, and administrators for the business of empire. SOAS' basement was full of missionary papers, the shelves of our libraries full of books written by white people about Africa.

The version of the slave trade that I heard as I grew up had emphasised the role of the British in first profiting from it and then in ending it. We were the protagonists. The villains and the saviours. I didn't know at that point that it took no less than twelve attempts over twenty-five years for the British government to finally legislate to end the slave trade. Nor that it was the anti-slavery movement that served as the bridgehead for the colonisation of West Africa. But I'm getting ahead of myself.

Piecing together the facts and figures gave me a whole new perspective on a past that was part of my present. It blew apart the simple story I'd grown up believing.

This is what I came to know.[14]

By 1770, at the height of their involvement, the British had control of around half of the slave trade from West Africa.[15]Slavery had become one of Britain's most profitable businesses.[16]

It's widely known that the conditions on board slave ships were cruel and dehumanising. What's less commonly acknowledged is the sheer scale of the lives so carelessly wasted and so cruelly taken. After hearing about the conditions on these ships in full gruesome detail, our British parliament did little more than recommend minor modifications to the size of the windows. The data shows that death rates on board remained high right to the very end of official British engagement in the trade. Records of ship manifests show that of the 3,259,441 for whom records of embarkation on British ships over the period of the slave trade exist, only 2,733,324 disembarked.[17] That is, more than half a million people - almost a fifth of all the passengers - perished on board British ships.

I crunched the numbers with a heavy heart, calculating percentages, and thinking about what this meant as a stain on the character of a country that basks in the conceit that we are a people who are above all fair and decent.

Taken as a whole, the registered death toll across slave ships run by the US, Spain, Portugal, Denmark, France, and Britain is a staggering 1,818,681 people.[18] This number is just what's on the official record. It doesn't include the contraband slave trade that continued all the way up to Brazil declaring the end of slavery in 1888, and quite possibly beyond. Nor does it include those who lost their lives in the 'factories' in which slaves were kept before transport, crammed together in dank cells without sanitation. Nor those who perished in the 'seasoning camps' when they arrived in the West Indies. Let alone those who were killed in the wars that led to so many people being enslaved at all.

The Atlantic slave trade was nothing less than genocide.

As British involvement in the slave trade intensified, British people bought into ownership of plantation slaves in the West Indies. It wasn't just the elite.[19] Many ordinary middle-class people bought into or inherited slave ownership from their relatives as a form of property and used it to get mortgages for their houses. As Nick Draper puts it, owning African slaves in the West Indies 'was routine, unexceptional and unexceptionable'.[20]

A detailed record now exists that shows the level of complicity of the British establishment. Reading Parliamentary debates, it was evident that much of the focus of opposition to ending the slave trade came from those with vested interests in the plantations of the West Indies.[21] The names of over a hundred MPs who held seats in Parliament between 1820 and 1835 can be found in the records of the commission who doled out compensation to the 46,000 slave owners who claimed it when slavery was finally banned in 1833.[22]

There was no compensation paid to the victims of slavery, mind. They didn't get a thing. It was those with blood on their hands, complicit in the miseries of enslavement who were paid, and quite handsomely too. Small fortunes. The amounts run into millions in today's money.

So, what changed things? Activism. (You know I'd say that.) It took a combination of taking to the courts, using petitions and the equivalent of social media of the time, and building alliances to get the politicians in Westminster to finally, *finally*, vote - on the 27th of March 1807 - in favour of the Slave Trade Act.

The story most white British people would tell you, if you asked them how the slave trade came to an end, is a drama involving only white male characters. Many British people would only be able to name one of them, William Wilberforce. Looking for landmarks, I came across a much more nuanced picture, one in which former slaves featured alongside influential members of the British judiciary and political elite and campaigners driven by the kind of religious motives that impel quite some number of today's white saviours.

One of those landmarks was the 1772 case of James Somerset, a slave who'd escaped and was recaptured and put on a boat to be returned to the West Indies. He was sitting in the docks in London aboard a ship bound for Jamaica when legal action was brought to free him arguing that there was nothing in British common law or any statutory law made by Parliament that recognised slavery. Behind this was Grenville Sharp, a civil servant and activist, who'd been looking for test cases that would challenge the legal justification for enslavement.

The judge, Lord Mansfield, ruled that slave owners could not legally force slaves to return to the colonies once they were in Britain; 'the state of slavery is,' he said, 'so odious, that nothing can be suffered to support it, but positive law'.[23] With this, those slaves who'd made it to Britain were free of coercion to return.

But this did not set them free.

The 1779 publication of a memoir of a former slave from eastern Nigeria, Olaudah Equiano was another. It became a bestseller. *The Interesting Narrative of the Life of Olaudah Equiano* told of his capture as a child, transport on a slave ship and eventual freedom. It played a pivotal role in raising public awareness of the horrors of slavery.[24]

In 1786, Equiano and other former slaves formed Britain's first Black political movement, Sons of Africa. Twelve Christian white men – nine Quakers and three Anglicans, including Grenville Sharp and Thomas Clarkson – formed, in 1787, The Society for Effecting the Abolition of the Slave Trade. Their aim was to influence parliament and raise public awareness. A concerted campaign began. Anti-slavery rallies were held. In 1788 alone, over 100 petitions were presented to the House of Commons.[25] Prominent supporters included Mary Wollstonecraft, author of the 1792 book *A Vindication of the Rights of Women.*

The son of the famous potter Wedgewood joined the campaign. His iconic image of a slave in chains with the question, "Am I not a man and a brother?" took the public by storm. It became the 18th century's best-known image of a Black person: the equivalent of an Instagram meme. Thomas Clarkson wrote, "ladies wore them in bracelets, and others had them fitted up in an ornamental manner as pins for their hair. At length the taste for wearing them became general, and thus fashion, which usually confines itself to worthless things, was seen for once in the honourable office of promoting the cause of justice, humanity and freedom".[26]

In 1791, evangelical Christian MP William Wilberforce got interested in the Society. In 1792 he first put to Parliament for the first time the legislation that would become the 1807 Slave Trade Act. On the twelfth attempt, driven through the

Commons and the Lords by the coalition of politicians who had come together in pursuit of this cause, it became law.

The Act has been celebrated as if it was the end of slavery. But I hadn't realised that the Parliamentary campaign had focused not slavery itself, but on the international traffic in persons. As I delved and delved, the story of the success of a social movement described as one of the greatest grassroots campaigns in British history started looking a bit more complex.

From what I read, it seemed that the passing of the 1807 Act had as much to do with geopolitics as morality. The French had been the first to pronounce a ban, spurred by the 1791 insurrection in Haiti and sealed by the 1794 French Revolution. What followed then was a diplomatic dance. Those pressing for and against abolition cited other countries in argument and counter argument, whilst British diplomats plied avenues of power, with imperial interests holding sway.[27]

In the debate in the Lords in February 1807 that eventually carried the Slave Trade Act through, Lord Grenville made not only the moral case. He also added a clever rhetorical move, casting the US as already *well on their way* to abolition - ahead of Britain.

> The United States of America, who had fixed the period of the abolition to take place in 1808, have anticipated that period (I wish we had had the glory of being the first in the race), and there is already, according to the last accounts, a bill in its unresisted progress through the legislature, for the immediate abolition of this trade.[28]

In fact, I found out when I took a closer look at the timing, it was the clause in the US Constitution prohibiting any stop to the importation of people before 1808 that was what was fixed. The US Congress was yet to vote the bill through.

In December 1806 Thomas Jefferson asked Congress to 'withdraw the citizens of the United States from all further participation in these violations of human rights'.[29] He seemed less concerned about the violation of human rights taking place on American soil; it was not until much later that the US brought its own internal slave trade in check. On the 2nd of March 1807, a bill was brought before US Congress and passed easily.

According to commentators, this was for pragmatic rather than moral reasons. There was a surplus of slaves, plenty enough for the use the Americans had for them, in the southern states.[30] The bill was signed into law on the 3rd of March, but because of the constitution, it wasn't until January 1st 1808 that the international slave trade was formally made a felony in the US.[31]

Not to be outdone by the Americans and recognising that the tide was turning – against a backdrop of the Napoleonic wars and the closing of French-controlled territories to British trade - the British parliament voted in favour of the Slave Trade Act, on March 27th 1807. Napoleon had re-introduced slavery in 1802, but France fell in line with the other European powers by 1815. Britain had set about negotiating bilateral treaties with European powers to end the trade, adopting the role of imperial broker that befit their globalising aspirations. By 1820, the US and all the major European powers – Holland, France, Spain, Sweden, Denmark, Austria, Russia along with the UK – had enacted the ban on the trade.

After 1807, Britain sent the navy to police the coast. From 1808 to 1860, 1,500 slaving ships were impounded and most of the 150,000 freed slaves were settled in the colony of Sierra Leone, where Christian missions had established schools, and were busy converting former slaves to Christianity.

I knew Sierra Leone had been a British colony. I'd assumed it had been annexed much as the British had established dominion along the West African coast and then carved up the territory with other European powers in 1885 as they sat in a conference room in Paris, drawing straight lines through towns, families and even people's houses, like the Oba whose house I visited on the Benin border. What I hadn't known was that Sierra Leone had been the focus in 1787 of a project to resettle Black Londoners living in poverty, the "Black Poor",[32] as the Conservative Prime Minister Pitt put it at the time so they "be no longer suffered to infest the streets of London".[33]

The "Province of Freedom" was established soon after, supported by anti-slavery campaigners who saw it as a way to engage former slaves in running the colony, lifting them out of poverty. The project was a failure, later denounced by Olaudah Equiano, who'd been enlisted in it at the outset. Britain went on to establish in 1808 the British Crown Colony of Sierra Leone on a small patch of land by the coast, with the port of Freetown serving as a base for the West Africa Squadron's patrol boats and as the capital of British West Africa.[34]

It was just the start of annexing land across West Africa. The British created and named countries that hadn't existed before, drew up borders, parcelled up territories as if they were theirs. And at that time, they were. There was a point when the British Empire held dominion over almost a quarter of the world's entire land area, the largest empire in history.

Slavery continued unabated. It wasn't outlawed by the British government for another 26 years, protecting the profiteers of slave labour on the sugar plantations of the West Indies. Many well-regarded members of the British establishment were amongst them, including the father of British Prime Minister William Gladstone, who in one of his first speeches as an MP in 1831 had argued in favour of compensation to slave owners.[35]

I'd been exposed to the British self-belief that it was a sense of morality rather than the economics of the emerging world system that led to the end of the trade. But it became clear, as I read, that it was only with waning fortunes of the sugar cane plantations of the Caribbean that the British government was willing to legislate to end slavery in 1833.

In 1944, a Trinidadian scholar who was to become the first Prime Minister of independent Trinidad and Tobago in 1962, Eric Williams, published a book called *Capitalism and Slavery* in the US, based on his Oxford University PhD thesis. It showed that the slave trade generated only small profits, relative to the sugar plantations serviced by it. Once the British Caribbean sugar industry fell into decline, he argued, it no longer served this purpose or the interests of those benefiting from this industry in the British parliament. The book had been spurned by UK publishers because the story he told so undermined the narrative that Britain had moved to end the slave trade for humanitarian reasons. It wasn't published in Britain until 1964.

I'd been led to believe that the 1833 Abolition of Slavery Act was the outcome of relentless pressure from humanitarian activists. But what if this was all just noise and the real reason for the government folding to their demands was a political calculus based on the falling value of sugar and the rising demand for lubricants for the machines that were fuelling the industrial revolution? Think green capitalism and today's booming market in 'plant-based' produce. Marketed as morality, it all made good business sense.

What were the politicians saying about all of this, I wondered? What swayed them? It was quite an eye-opener to dip into the Parliamentary record in Hansard and tune into the debates. I could visualise the larded gentry sitting on those wooden benches, just like the William Reese-Moggs of today, and scoffing as anti-slavery campaigners unleashed a litany of the miseries being inflicted on slaves in Britain's colonies.

One debate stood out: on May 15th, 1823, the MP Thomas Fowell Buxton made a speech arguing for the atonement that Britain is yet to make – Tony Blair's statement of regret in 2007 having fallen short of an apology, skirting the question of reparations.[36]

For all the blood spilt in African wars fomented by English capital—

for civil war which we contrived to render interminable—for all the villages set in flames-by the contending parties—for all the horrors and the terrors of these poor creatures, roused from their rest by the yells of the man-hunter whom we sent—for civilization excluded—for the gentle arts which embellish life excluded—for honest and harmless commerce excluded—for Christianity, and all that it comprehends, expelled for two centuries from Africa—for the tens and tens of thousands of men murdered in these midnight marauds—for the tens and tens of thousands suffocated in the holds of our slave-ships—for the tens and tens of thousands of emaciated beings, cast ashore in the West Indies, emaciated beings, "refuse men" (for such was the mercantile phrase) lingering to a speedy death—for the tens and tens of thousands still more unhappy who, surviving, lived on to perpetual slavery, to the whip of the taskmaster, to ignorance, to crime, to heathen darkness—for all these, we owe large and liberal atonement.[37]

You'd think that this might have swayed people. Reading the debate, though, it was clear that there wasn't much morality to go around. The question of compensation became the sticking point. [39] When the Abolition of Slavery Act was finally passed in 1833, the terms were dear. A £20m loan was taken to pay off British slave owners – equivalent to at least £16bn today and representing 40% of the Treasury's annual income at the time.

Three words stood out from Thomas Buxton's speech, words that framed British intervention and ultimately gave moral license and economic motive to colonisation – civilisation, commerce, and Christianity.

In 1939, Buxton founded The Society for the Extinction of the Slave Trade and for the Civilization of Africa.[40] In that same year, he published a 522-page long book, *The African Slave Trade and Its Remedy*. It was evident that the banning of slavery and the West Africa Squadron's naval efforts were having little effect. He writes:

For every village fired and every drove of human beings marched in former times, there are now double. For every cargo at sea, two cargoes, or twice the number in one cargo, wedged together in a mass of living corruption, are now borne on the wave of the Atlantic.[41]

Buxton's remedy? A journey along the Niger river to sign

anti-slavery treaties with local rulers, promote Christianity, agriculture, and 'legitimate trade' to replace the trade in slaves. The 1841 Niger Expedition was an abject failure. But on one of the boats was a man whose influence came to shape what would become Nigeria and the people who would become Yoruba.

The Reverend Samuel Ajayi Crowther was a polymath linguist born in Osogun, in the Oyo empire, captured by a raid by Muslim Fulani in 1822 when he was ten and traded for a horse, some wine and tobacco to Portuguese traders in Lagos. Shackled with irons on a slave boat bound for the Americas, he was freed by the British squadron and settled in Sierra Leone, where he was converted to Christianity. He translated the Bible into Yoruba, a project that took him 40 years. Crowther returned to Nigeria as Africa's first Black Bishop to oversee the work of proselytization seen by the British as the principal remedy for slavery.

Earlier in my time in Nigeria, I'd wondered, 'whose Yoruba culture am I writing about?'. The answer, I realised, was that 'Yoruba' wasn't an identity people would give to themselves. Yoruba was the language they spoke, in different dialects. The people I got to know identified with towns or sub-groups - Egbados, Aworis, Egbas, Ijeshas. Samuel Crowther brought together the Yoruba as a single people and gave them a holy book in a standardised script, with which they could be colonised.

I'd gone to Nigeria with an assumption that Christianity had been spread by white people. It was the same assumption that made people think I must be a missionary. In fact, African missionaries like Bishop Crowther were far more effective agents of Christian conversion.[41] Returnee former slaves from Sierra Leone called *sàró* had been converted to Christianity in Sierra Leone's mission stations and schools. They were then recruited as missionaries and administrators to service the colonising ambitions of the British Empire.

From the 1830s, *sàrós* began to return to Nigeria. They brought trading connections along the coast and a sense of new economic possibilities. And they became the bridgehead of the incipient colonial power. I learnt how they'd been deployed to the towns of the interior to promote Christianity and commercial agriculture, introducing new cash crops, opening mission stations, and founding churches and schools.

Returnee slaves from Brazil, àgùdà, began coming home too. Adédoyin Tèriba suggests that by 1880, ten percent of the population of Lagos were Brazilian or Cuban returnee slaves.[42] They brought with them ingredients for favourite foods Nigerians now eat every day – cassava, tomato, Scotch bonnet pepper – and food processing techniques, especially important for cyanide-rich cassava.[43] Those vats of fermenting cassava outside my window wafting their putrid smell into my room were part of the process of making it safe to eat.

The cultural imprint of the returnee Brazilian àgùdà brought dynamism to Lagos and opened up new lines of transatlantic trade. The imprint of the Sierra Leone returnee sàró was more indelible: the innumerable Church Missionary Society agents who fanned out through the interior did the British Empire's work, accomplishing Buxton's remedy. The Church Missionary Society put it directly: "The opening up of Nigeria to Christian mission originated in the desire of British merchants to extend their trade on the West Africa coast."[44]

For this, CMS African missionaries were to experience the indignity of being turfed out of their jobs by a generation of white missionaries who believed that they could do things better. Samuel Crowther, distressed by having his work discredited, died of a stroke in 1891. He was replaced by a white Bishop.[45] Funso Aiyejina talks of how the Christian recruits

... became a new generation of middle-men and women who functioned as arrowheads for the denigration of African cultures. So, while a number of pre-colonial African chiefs and merchants betrayed their fellow Africans by selling them into enslavement, the intellectual

Crowthers, acting as priests, interpreters, translators, policemen, postmasters, and schoolteachers were key players in the process of the religious, psychological and mental enslavement of African peoples.[46]

I'd grown up believing the anti-slavery movement to be a triumph of humanitarianism and human rights. But uncovering the story, I came to realise how for the British Empire, it provided the springboard for the incremental annexation of territories so large that by 1914, they could declare the birth of the Nigeria they had created.

A CONSIDERATION WHICH HAS FAILED

All this got me thinking about the legacy for Ilemi of those long years of insecurity. Imagine growing up with the fear that when you venture outside the town, marauding gangs could threaten you with a gun and drag you off with them. Imagine getting married in a different town from your mum and dad and knowing that if you went to see them or they came to see you, walking the smooth, hardened red earth trails that wove through brilliant forest green, 'full of antelopes, monkeys, red-tailed parrots, and Guinea hens' – as T.J. Bowen, the American Baptist Missionary who travelled through the area at the time, described it - there was always that risk that you or they wouldn't make it home again.[47]

So many people disappeared. So much trauma, sadness, and loss. So much suffering. This went on for years and years, so long that a child born in the times the Ọ̀yọ́ Empire collapsed might fear their grandchildren would be captured and trafficked by slavers if they left the town. Because it was so dangerous, women travelled in large groups for safety. Even the little markets sounded large, and the big ones were huge, attracting thousands of buyers and sellers. All those bargains netted some women fortunes. An elaborate system of tolls worked a bit like the roadblocks that peppered the border area. Smugglers like the *fayawo* boys worked the rivers and lagoons.

Ilemi's elders had built a great big protective wall around the town and dug a trench to shield the townspeople from capture. For almost twenty years, the town was under siege by their neighbours. They'd said it was so hazardous to venture beyond its bounds, men had neglected their farms. Only older women were able to move freely, and I was told they did so in large groups, trading up and down the corridors from the interior to the sea.

By the time the siege ended in 1853, the CMS missionary Samuel Crowther recorded in his journal the town as being 'in a miserable condition' and 'bearing the distress of war and the appearance of desolation'.[48] But gradually Ilemi bounced back. Traders and refugees came and settled, turning the town into a thriving centre for trade on the routes that ran inland and to the coast.

Although if I was honest with myself, I lacked the rigour or the patience of a historian, I loved sleuthing in the archives thumbing through the records left behind by the missionaries and visitors to the region. Through this new lens, I found their diaries and the impressions they'd chosen to record intriguing. I'd begun treating them anthropologically, as I would a people with whom I was not familiar and about whom I wanted to gain an understanding. It made me much less harshly judgemental, more curious. Even when my prejudices were making my hackles rise, I found in the exercise of an anthropological sensibility something close to the possibility of empathy.

One of the books I re-read in this way was the American Baptist Missionary T. J. Bowen's *Adventures and Missionary Labours in Several Countries in the Interior of Africa from 1849 to 1856*. I found out all kinds of interesting things from the missionary's observations concerning women. I learnt, for example, that more than half of the Dahomean army who attacked Ilemi from the West were women, trained from childhood, celibate and treated to copious amounts of tobacco and alcohol.[49]

It was in his accounts of institutions like masquerades and markets that I found some of the most vivid images of the women of those times. He told of how when a particularly scary masquerade, *oro*, was brought out, women were forced to stay cooped up inside. This was a recipe, by his account, for ten thousand arguments. You get from his description of what happened once the women left the streets such a strong sense of how integral women's trade was to the everyday life of the town, including the sale of ready-made food to spare women the work of preparing the evening meal:

> Now and then some poor fellow, with a pot of water on his head, slipped through the streets, as if ashamed, and crept into the closed house, where his wife was to use the water in preparing his dinner. Several little boys, and some big ones, were seen with provisions, etc., to sell, but they had an awkward sheepish air about them, never attempted the usual cries of "hot yams!", "sweet sauce!" etc., and were clearly inadequate to the smiles and chat of the girls, whose places they were endeavouring to fill.[50]

That these women were no shrinking violets is clear from the description he gives of a market just north of Ilemi. Bowen writes:

> The principal marketing hour, and the proper time to see all the wonders, is in the evening. At half an hour before sunset, all sorts of people, men, women, girls, travelers lately arrived in the caravans, farmers from the fields, and artizans from their houses, are pouring in from all directions to buy and sell and talk. At the distance of half a mile their united voices roar like the waves of the sea. The women, especially, always noisy, are then in their glory, bawling out salutations, cheapening and higgling, conversing, laughing, and sometimes quarreling, with a shrillness and compass of voice which indicates both their determination and their ability to make themselves heard. As the shades of evening deepen, if the weather allows the market to continue, and there is no moon, every woman lights her little lamp, and presently the market presents to the distant observer, the beautiful appearance of innumerable bright stars.[51]

I read Bowen's words with a smile of recognition. I'd sat in my little hiding place on the roof so many times, listening to the hubbub of chatter and greetings and looking out at the streets around the market lined with hawkers with their little lamps twinkling in the night as dusk fell.

One way to get rich quick in that era was contraband in humans. Amongst the most successful slave traders were women from the elite, wives of kings or well-connected sole traders who had the economic and political connections to borrow on credit and navigate trade route tolls and the hazards of travel. I remember chancing on drummers high in the cobbled colonial streets of the old Brazilian town of Olinda one night, in the middle of the carnival, and hearing the chants of singers celebrating the Alaafin of Ọ̀yọ́ in broken Yoruba. A chill ran through my very being. The Alaafin's wives were legendary slave traders; the Ọ̀yọ́ Empire was at the very heart of the growth of the Atlantic slave trade until it fell apart at the end of the 18th century.[52] Its dissolution led to the enslavement of tens of thousands more.

I read stories in the historical record of legendary women who'd made it big. There was a time when I would have claimed for them the status of feminist heroine. Now I was a bit more circumspect. They'd empowered themselves, that was for sure. But at whose cost? One of these women was Efunsetan Aniwura, *Ìyàlóde* of Ibadan's market and an influential political figure. She'd taken against the British and ended up the wrong side of the ruler of Ibadan. He'd commissioned her murder by two of her own slaves. They'd entered her room through the ceiling – much as the lads in the room next to me had done, I imagine - and bludgeoned her to death.

By the mid-nineteenth century, Efunsetan is said to have accumulated two thousand slaves of her own, using them to transport goods up and down the trade corridors to the growing city-state of Ibadan, to ports including Badagry and nearby Porto Novo, to farm and to develop products for the growing market economy of Ibadan. She was described by one CMS missionary, in 1853, as 'a woman of acute judgement and manly courage'.[53] I thought of the women in Ilemi who talked of women who had 'became a man', like the legendary *Ìyà* Kotu.

Another celebrated woman trader was Madam Efunporoye Tinubu. She traded slaves for tobacco and guns and became a hugely influential business tycoon and political operator. Outmanoeuvred by the British Consul of Lagos, who she'd challenged, she was banished to Abeokuta where she rose to great influence, including as *Ìyàlóde* of Abeokuta's huge market.[54] Like *Ìyà* Galura, she'd started with gathering roots and leaves to trade.

I couldn't imagine women like these being bossed around by any man.

Efunsetan and Madam Tinubu each had a string of husbands. I read of the daughters of kings and chiefs of this era being free to take lovers. The colonial ethnographer A.B. Ellis, who'd documented the fabulous story of Ilemi being founded in the place where the goddess Odudua ravished the handsome hunter, wrote of how most young women had lovers in secret. I'd added this to the feminist fable I was busy constructing in my mind at the time.

It would be hard to imagine a bigger gap between a past in which women were so empowered they accumulated huge fortunes, brokered war and peace, and took lovers whenever they felt like it and a present so filled with talk of 'endurance' and the litany of 'uselessing' and 'uselessness'.

And there was more.

On one of my trips to the archives in Ibadan, I'd stumbled across the leather bound Badagry District Commissioner's Civil Record Book from 1887-1894. It was filled with cases, recorded in neat, flowing blue handwriting. Many involved women brought before the District Commissioner for 'A Consideration Which Has Failed'. The consideration was the long, drawn-out process that led from *itoro* to *idana*, engagement ceremony to wedding.

The transcripts detailed payments of cowries - the shells that had come to be used as currency - gin and cloth and acts of labour such as mending the roof. These were reclaimed when arrangements broke down, neatly itemised, and translated into cash reimbursements. Amongst them was the 1892 case of one woman so spirited in her own defence and so pointed in her cross-examination of the man who'd brought her there, she grabbed my imagination. Her name was Abesi, her husband Onikoye, and a snatch of the dialogue faithfully transcribed in English by the court clerk went like this:

Abesi: 'When I agreed to be your wife, did not my father tell you that I had had connection with a man?'

Onikoye: 'No'.

Abesi: 'Did my father not send me to Lagos and did I not live there for some time as your wife?'

Onikoye: 'Yes but came to see my people and you were young then and did not live as my wife.'

Abesi: 'When I returned to Badagry and you asked me to go back with you to Lagos, did I not tell you that I did not like your ways, so would not go with you?'

Onikoye: 'No.'

Abesi: 'Did I not tell you that if you wished to be my husband, I would be your wife at Badagry, not at Lagos?'

Giving as good as she got, Abesi got off without having to pay anything back. I visualised her in one of those high-ceilinged whitewashed colonial buildings with dark wood beams and heavy, formal mahogany furniture, standing straight-backed and defiant as she faced her former husband and gave him what for.

In the district commissioner's record book, I also came across lots of other cases that told a story of women in control of their own money. It was clear that women were making enough cash to sort out the repayments themselves. The traces left behind were of women who were seeking their own pleasures and calling the shots in their relationships.

What hadn't occurred to me at the time was the possibility that the timeless 'traditional' past that I was being told about, a past that stretched beyond the borders of remembered time, wasn't just a narrative fiction used to chastise young people. I'd taken the court cases, the writings of Ellis and the epidemiological record from the early colonial period, which revealed high levels of sexually transmitted diseases. They'd added up to what seemed to me to be an unspeakable truth about the past. *N'igba atijo* became, in this reading, the stuff of fable; it seemed to speak more to present anxieties about women's sexuality than about an actual past.

But then a thought sparked in my mind, making connections that I just hadn't seen before. I began putting all of this together.

Until the late 18th century, I'd found out, it was relatively rare for men to have lots of wives. Polygamy was only really for chiefs and kings. But in the wrecked social landscape that was left behind after decades of war and the predations of slavers, women slaves were absorbed as wives into families. They and their children were used as labour as appetite for European goods drove the expansion of cash crops.

One of the reasons men could accumulate so many wives was that they didn't need to bother providing for them or their children. As Samuel Johnson had documented in his *History of the Yorubas*, men would be expected to give women 'starting capital' to set them up in business, but the profit belonged to her. This added up to a situation in which women weren't just providing for themselves and their kids. Some were also sustaining men with their earnings. This had been going on for generations. It was as traditional as it gets.

So, what was going on with all those stories of chaste, docile girls who became faithful, domesticated wives? There was a place that this came from. The patriarchal fantasies of the Christian missionaries, who'd played such a decisive role in the colonisation of the country. Part of their agenda had been to actively promote a nuclear family unit in which women were subservient to men. They'd written in their journals of their ambitions to bring about the subordination of women, turning spirited, mouthy women like Abesi into good Christian wives who would quietly obey and *endure*.

It can't have been easy. Yoruba women were no push-over. Baptist missionary Bowen sums up the challenge the missionaries had on their hands:

> Men, of course, have the privilege of divorcing their wives, and the matter is made all the easier from the fact that every woman is a free-dealer, who labours for herself and supports herself and has no claim on her husband's property. . . is sole owner of her property and earnings, [and] is not obliged to work for her husband and has no claim on him for support, either for herself or her children.[55]

For British and American missionaries, this level of independence was completely out of kilter with the expectations instilled in them by their own culture. This was after, all, an era in which women were not supposed to have any thoughts of their own, let alone their own income and property.

The missionaries were also the harbingers of Husbands. Bowen went on to observe, in his comments on women's economic autonomy:

> In this way the man escapes the burden of supporting his wives and children.[56]

Those very attitudes and mores leached into the mindsets and writings of Yoruba missionaries, especially those who'd come of age in Christian mission schools. Johnson and his fellow countrymen brought back from Sierra Leone attitudes about women and men that were utterly foreign to the context in which they worked. Their work as agents of Christian evangelism was to shape a future that would become the idealised *n'igba atijo* I'd be told about a hundred years later.

It felt that I'd come full circle. I'd gone to Nigeria fuelled with a feminist fantasy of a society in which women were treated very differently to the Britain I'd grown up in. Enchanted by anthropologists and art historians' tales of rites and rituals that honoured the elemental powers of women, I'd gone in search of inspiration from a society that I believed to have the kind of gender relations that feminists of my mother's generation had begun waging a battle for that was still raging. I'd brought with me the rich mythology that slaves from this region had carried to Brazil and reinvented there as a mode of resistance and survival, stories of amazing goddesses who were defiant, brilliant, outspoken, and brave. I wanted to believe a world was possible in which there were no subordinate wives whose only power was to be found in acts of defiance, like my mother's friend who whipped off the tablecloth and drenched her husband in gravy.

How important it had been to me to find something other to 'my culture', in that far-away place. How distraught I'd been to find that the project I'd so carefully constructed was all an elaborate fiction brewed up in the head of a wishful young white woman reading about mystical Africa in the teal coloured, carpeted aisles of a colonial-era British university library. But what I found once I let go of my flawed project was something that I might never otherwise have brought into view and sought to understand. I met women whose courage, strength and resilience were inspiring. But I also came to see the legacy of colonialism close up and personal. And it changed everything for me, as a white person interested in the wider world and in social justice.

Looking back, abanoning my project was the best thing that happened to me. The journey of discovery that I embarked on taught me more about the human condition than any of the schemes I might have come up with in advance and allowed to shape my fieldwork. It brought me back to an anthropology that I'd only vaguely known to be possible before, one deeply rooted in what it means to be human. Getting lost meant that what I found was more precious, more meaningful. I came to realise that if I hadn't gone on that excursion, if I hadn't had to redefine my purpose, I might well have found it harder to find what I did end up learning. It taught me a lesson that's stayed with me: when researchers impose onto their fields of study the questions that they think ought to be asked, the chances are that they'll miss what's right under their noses.

THE GOODBYE PARTY

It was only when I watched the video afterwards that I became aware of just how long they'd waited. It hadn't been intended as part of the commission, but the camera captured my delay. I saw guests filing in, dressed in the best guinea brocade and lace, as the low-slung sun painted the sky with dazzling streaks of apricot, fuchsia and scarlet. The cameraman panned across the concrete rooftop, taking in the rows of white plastic chairs and the party lights being rigged up ready for my arrival.

Hours later, the guests were flagging. The glare of the lights lit up sections of the roof. Others were submerged into the deepening gloom of a moonless night. The excited hubbub brought by the guests had quietened into a steady state of waiting. Cicadas dominated the soundscape. The children were hungry and had to be fed. The large bowls of jollof rice were losing heat, the stew to spoon over them congealing.

Stanley hadn't accompanied me on this, my final journey. Chastened by the risk of breaking down, I'd borrowed a little light blue Toyota from the nuns to run up to Ibadan to get my passport and say my goodbyes. Things were getting feisty in Lagos. A cancelled election. A military ruler who'd promised to leave, to let the transition to democracy happen. And then the powers that held the country in a fragile equilibrium pulled back.

Our basement had been a nerve centre for the politicos of the town over the tense hours during which the vote had been counted, messages coming in from across the region of likely victory. A Yoruba win. One that would shift the balance of power in the country, pulling it away from the northern military elite. And then the temerity of annulling the election. Hope snatched so cruelly away. There were rumours of riots spilling out from Lagos along the road from Ikeja to Ota, fears that the airport would be closed.

"I'll be fine here," I'd said, "I feel safe. I'll just keep a low profile. I am sure it will blow over. We're far enough from Lagos."

"You must go," said Bayo. "Who knows what will happen. This could be the start of a civil war. People have had enough."

I'd just figured out what it was that I was doing. Now wasn't the time to pack up and go. It was Grace who pointed out my foolishness. I could stay and stay and then suddenly things could flare up, and I wouldn't be able to leave.

By the time I left for the airport, protests had ignited Ijeka and its roads were barely navigable. We drove through crowds brandishing leafy branches, shouting "IBB 419, Maryam drug dealer!". IBB was President Ibrahim Babangida, who was supposed to be leaving office. And 419 was the article in the criminal code concerning fraud, associated with a scam finessed by Nigerian scammers of spinning a yarn in order to empty someone's bank account. Maryam, IBB's wife, was widely rumoured to be using the diplomatic bag to run a thriving cocaine smuggling business. People were angry. Led down the garden path of an end to military rule, only to find the army at the end of it.

I kept my window wound down and a smile on my face as we moved through the throng. To be an *oyinbo* fleeing in fear felt like the very worst way to leave the country that had taken me in and indulged me so very generously and graciously.

As it turned out, I reached the airport minutes before it closed.

I spent hours enclosed there with an anxious throng. People were clutching small radios to their ears to catch the news that was coming in via the BBC World Service of the riots spreading through Lagos, calling out regular updates. Others pressed their faces up against the large airport windows, the atmosphere thick with spiralling black clouds of burning tyres.

Eventually, Air France sent in a couple of large planes and lifted us all out.

But all that was ahead of me at the point when we drew up to the house, weary from the long ride to and from Ibadan. The route had taken us through towns that normally bustled with traffic, now stilled into an eery quiet. Everyone was waiting for something to happen. It had still taken the best part of a day to go there and back to Ibadan, and it was now pitch dark. I looked up in surprise at the lights on the roof and caught the tops of the white lines of chairs. A cheer went up. Suddenly I could hear chair legs scraping on the concrete and see people peering down at us, and waving.

"Auntie Ann!", little Tade was so excited he was jumping up and down, "your party is ready! We've been waiting!".

Before I could join the guests, Grace told me, I needed to make myself fine. There would be a video. As I pulled off my dusty *buba* and wrapper, I cast a critical eye over the rail with the collection of garments I'd acquired over the year. None were quite right for the occasion. My Mrs Mainstream flowery dresses were by now threadbare rags. The designer outfits Grace had her tailor make for me were limp and pallid. The harsh *kongi* soap I'd hand-washed them with in the big washing vat by the tap at the bottom of our back yard had taken the colour and texture out of them.

At the end of the row was my money-bank *buba* and wrapper, still beautiful, with its bright blue hues. I'd taken the last but one $100 to Ibadan with me, bringing back a large paper bag full of

Naira to give as parting gifts.

I put it on.

"Come and help me do my head-tie," I called to Grace, who was commandeering the team running to and from the kitchen with re-heated food.

I'd never mastered the twists and ties that would make the elaborate confections that she could create with a flick of her wrist. Grace took hold of the long length of cloth. It was the one under the cover of which I'd travelled in search of a fieldsite all those months ago, my whiteness safely concealed. She did me proud.

Resplendent, I emerged from my room. As I climbed the concrete steps to the roof, I was met with a voluble chorus of talking drums singing my praises. A warm wave of applause rippled around me. Steaming hot dishes of my favourite food, *egusi ati iyan*, were quickly placed before the hungry guests. The sound system brought the party to life with Fela, fuji and funk. And we danced, deep into the night.

POSTSCRIPT

Being Human began with a couple of the funnier incidents described here, written for my daughter Kate who had insisted I write them down for her. Kate went travelling and sent me a message one day to tell me she was getting interested in anthropology and wondering whether to study it at university. I set myself a project: to write up the stories into a book and send it to her as a Christmas present to read on her Kindle on long bus journeys.

There was something that wasn't right about telling what I'd come to refer to as "my Stanley stories" in isolation from a larger narrative that explains what I was doing there in the first place. I found myself reflecting on some of the things I'd taken for granted about being an anthropologist. It also made me think about the things I'd questioned at the time, but hadn't felt there was sufficient space in the discipline to voice. The decolonising movement has now made this kind of auto-critique possible.

What this book has become is as much a story about anthropology, about the practice of fieldwork and the experience of doing a PhD, as about Stanley and his adventures. In the process of writing it, I've thought deep and hard about what it means to speak about Africa from a subject position as a white anthropologist in these times, and about how important it is to do so from a perspective of critical self-accountability.

There was a moment whilst writing when I visualised myself standing in the sea on Badagry beach gazing at the horizon.

I realised my knowledge of the slave trade and its impact on Africa was vestigial. I held that thought while I researched what it was that I should have known. For weeks, I immersed myself in everything I could find. Ship manifest records, Parliamentary proceedings, lists of slave owners requesting compensation, missionary memoirs, a thesis from 1944 that had so challenged the orthodoxies peddled by the British that it wasn't published in the UK for two decades and only recently rediscovered. I pieced together a story that I simply hadn't heard told before, one that profoundly challenged the narrative about the slave trade that I'd grown up believing. For the political education of engaging with all of this alone, this was a book worth writing.

Revisiting my experiences in Nigeria has made me reflect on the humanizing potential of anthropological fieldwork. It's made me think about what might happen if more people - especially people in public service and in the management and administration of institutions like universities - were to immerse themselves in the everyday realities of those whom they are there to serve. Ultimately, this book has taken me back to what attracted me to anthropology in the first place: to understand what it means to be human. I hope that it offers those who, like Kate, are thinking about studying anthropology, some insight into what anthropologists do - and a cautionary warning to do your homework before you set out.

THANKS

There are so many people to thank, I don't know where to start. First of all, I'd like to express my deepest gratitude and love to the people who appear in this book with the names of Grace, Margaret, Bayo, Ayomide, Bolanle, Tade and Bisi. Thank you for taking me in and for all your care. Baba Tinu, you are missed. Iya Dayo, I owe you a huge debt for putting up with my often ridiculous questions and for subjecting you to all that walking around town.

To the many people in Ilemi who indulged this *alejo* and her many questions, a warm thanks. I don't feel I ever did justice to the time you gave me so generously. My supervisors were amazing, and as I'm writing this incognito, I am not naming them here, but my debt to them remains massive.

Kate, I wouldn't have written this if it hadn't been for you. Writing this for you has made it so much enjoyable. Jake, I think this proves decisively what you've always suspected about anthropologists and their ways. Ian, that Rastaman in the apricot suit was so right. TC, my gratitude for all you've taught me about what it means to be human. And Orkideh, thank you. I wouldn't have persisted if you hadn't insisted.

READINGS

I'm going to divide these readings into two categories. The first are books that changed the way I see the world, most of them written by anthropologists. I'd love for you to read them, they might also change the way you see your world. The second are books and articles I've referred to here, that you might want to pick up and read for yourself.

****

Must-Reads

Talal Asad, 1973, *Anthropology and the Colonial Encounter*, New York: Humanities Press.

Ruth Behar, 1997, *The Vulnerable Observer: Anthropology that Breaks Your Heart*, Boston: Beacon Press.

Robert Borofsky, 2019, *An Anthropology of Anthropology: Is It Time to Shift Paradigms*, Kailua, HI: Center for Public Anthropology.

Pierre Bourdieu, 1984, *Distinction: A Social Critique of the Judgement of Taste*, Cambridge, MA: Harvard University Press.

Robert Chambers, 1983, *Rural Development: Putting the Last First*, London: Routledge.

Patricia Hill Collins, 1990, *Black Feminist Thought*, Boston: Unwin Hyman.

Felicia Ekejiuba, 1995, 'Down to Fundamentals: Women-centred Hearth-holds in Rural West Africa', in *Women Wielding the Hoe*, ed. Deborah Bryceson, London: Routledge.

Paul Gilroy, 1993, *The Black Atlantic: Modernity and Double Consciousness*, Cambridge, MA: Harvard University Press.

Nelson Goodman, 1978, *Ways of Worldmaking*, Hassocks: Harvester Press.

Kate Fox, 2005, *Watching the English: The Hidden Rules of English Behaviour*, London: Hodder and Stoughton.

Stuart Hall, 1986, 'The problem of ideology. Marxism without guarantees', *Journal of Communication Inquiry*, 10(2): 28–44.

Zora Neale Hurston, 1937, *Their Eyes Were Watching God*, Philadelphia: J.P. Lippincott & Co.

Michael Jackson, 1989, *Paths Toward a Clearing: Radical Empiricism and Ethnographic Inquiry*, Bloomington: Indiana University Press.

Lisa Lindsay, 1996, *Putting the Family on Track: Gender and Domestic Life on the Colonial Nigerian Railway*, Ph.D. dissertation: University of Michigan, Ann Arbor, Michigan

Obioma Nnaemeka, 1996, *Sisterhood, Feminisms, and Power: From Africa to the Diaspora*. Trenton, NJ: Africa World Press.

Omolara Ogundipe-Leslie, 1994, *Recreating Ourselves: African Women and Critical Transformations*, Trenton, NJ: Africa World Press.

Renato Rosaldo, 2014, 'Grief and the Headhunter's Rage', in *The Day of Shelly's Death: The Poetry and Ethnography of Grief*, Durham, N.C.: Duke University Press.

Nancy Scheper-Hughes, 1993, *Death Without Weeping: The Violence of Everyday Life in Brazil*, Berkeley: University of California Press.

Cornel West, 1988, 'Marxist theory and the specificity of Afro-American oppression', in Cary Nelson and Lawrence Grossman (eds.), *Marxism and the Interpretation of Cultures*, Urbana: University of Illinois Press.

Raymond Williams, 1976, *Keywords: A Vocabulary of Culture and Society*, London: Croom Helm.

References

T. J. Bowen, 1857, *Adventures and Missionary Labours in Several Countries in the Interior of Africa from 1849 to 1856*, Charleston: Southern Baptist Publication Society.

Thomas Fowell Buxton, 1839, *The African Slave Trade and Its Remedy*, London: John Murray.

Henry Drewal and Margaret Thompson Drewal, 1983, *Gelede: Art and Female Power Among the Yoruba*, Bloomington: Indiana University Press.

Michael Drinkwater, 1991, 'Visible actors and visible researchers: critical hermeneutics in an actor-oriented perspective', unpublished paper.

Alfred Burdon Ellis, 1894, *The Yoruba-speaking peoples of the Slave Coast of West Africa*, London: Chapman and Hall.

E.P. Evans-Pritchard, 1940, *The Nuer: A Description of the Modes of Livelihood and Political Institutions of a Nilotic People*, Oxford: Clarendon.

James Frazer, 1890, *The Golden Bough: A Study in Comparative Religion*, London: Macmillan and Co.

Clifford Geertz, 1973, *The Interpretation of Cultures*, New York: Basic Books.

Samuel Johnson, 1921, *The History of the Yorubas: From the Earliest Times to the Beginning of the British Protectorate*, Cambridge: Cambridge University Press.

Claude Lévi-Strauss, 1978, *Myth and Meaning*, London: Routledge & Kegan Paul.

Jamie Bruce Lockhart and Paul Lovejoy, 2005, *Hugh Clapperton into the Interior of Africa: Records of the Second Expedition 1825-1827*, Leiden: Brill.

Martin Lynn, 1997, *Commerce and Economic Change in West Africa: The Palm Oil Trade in the Nineteenth Century*, Cambridge: Cambridge University Press.

Bronislaw Malinowski, 1922, *Argonauts of the Southern Pacific*, London: Routledge.

Martin Meredith, 2016, *The Fortunes of Africa: A 5000-Year History of Wealth, Greed and Endeavor*, New York: Public Affairs.

Lewis Henry Morgan (edited by Leslie White), 1993, *The Indian Journals 1859-1862*, New York: Dover Publications.

J.D.Y. Peel, 2000, *Religious Encounter and the Making of the Yoruba*, Indian University Press, Bloomington.

Pertti Pelto and Gretel Pelto, 1978, *Anthropological Research The Structure of Inquiry*, Cambridge: Cambridge University Press.

Annette B. Weiner, 1988, *The Trobrianders of Papua New Guinea*, New York: Holt, Rinehart and Winston.

Pierre Verger, 1985, *Fluxo e Refluxo do Tráfico de Escravos entre o Golfo de Benin e a Bahia de Todos os Santos.* Salvador: Corrupio.

Tom Wengraf, 2001, *Qualitative Research Interviewing: Biographic Narrative and Semistructured Method*, London: Sage.

Notes

1.   https://aladdynking.com/ghana-must-go-the-ugly-history-of-africas-

most-famous-bag/

2. At the time, calling my car Stanley was an ironic nod to the adventurer who traversed the continent - these being the days before a decolonising consciousness would descend on me and make such a choice unthinkable, let alone the fact that the man was a Christian missionary. But Stanley he was named and it would be unfair to pretend otherwise.

3. J. A. Barnes, 1962, 'African Models in the New Guinea Highlands,' *Man*, 62:5-9.

4. Bronislaw Malinowski, 1930, 'Practical Anthropology,' Africa: Journal of the International African Institute, January 1929, Vol. 2, No. 1, pp 22-38, p. 27.

5. Tom Wengraf, 2001, *Qualitative Research Interviewing: Biographic Narrative and Semistructured Method*, London: Sage Publications.

6. Martin Lynn, 1997, *Commerce and Economic Change in West Africa: The Palm Oil Trade in the Nineteenth Century*, Cambridge: Cambridge University Press. Pauline von Hellerman, 'Red Gold: A History of Palm Oil in West Africa,' https://chinadialogue.net/en/food/red-gold-a-history-of-palm-oil-in-west-africa/ January 18th, 2021.

7. Paul Gilroy, 1993, *The Black Atlantic: Modernity and Double Consciousness*, Cambridge, Mass.: Harvard University Press.

8. Pierre Verger, 1985, *Fluxo e Refluxo do Trafico de Escravos entre o Golfo de Benin e a Bahia de Todos os Santos*, Salvador: Corrupio.

9. http://wayback.archive-it.org/10611/20180706175055/; http://www.unesco.org/new/fileadmin/MULTIMEDIA/HQ/CLT/pdf/MapSlaveRoute.pdf

10. Quite a few of these old books have now been digitised and it's interesting to read them by searching them with keywords. Try putting 'woman' into this one: https://archive.org/details/yorubacountry00hinduoft

11. Jamie Bruce Lockhart and Paul Lovejoy, *Hugh Clapperton into the Interior of Africa: Records of the Second Expedition 1825-1827*, Leiden: Brill.

12. Samuel Johnson, 1921, *The History of the Yorubas: From the Earliest Times to the Beginning of the British Protectorate*, Cambridge: Cambridge University Press.

13. https://www.revolutionaryplayers.org.uk/the-first-manufacturing-town-industry-in-birmingham-in-the-mid-19th-century-the-new-illustrated-directory-1858/

14. I take some liberties here with a rather cheeky use of the ethnographic present. I came to know some of this in the time before the internet, before Catherine Hall's Legacies of British Slavery and the Slave Voyages project, before the digitisation of Hansard, before the books written by Paul Lovejoy, Martin Meredith, Toby Green and all the others from whom I learned so much as I wrote this book. I include these links and all this detail for you, Kate, fledgling historian, to do your own homework on this terrible, shameful history in which we are implicated as white British people. I include all this, too, because I am angry that I was sold a lie as I grew up and because of

the disgrace I feel as someone who is British about my country never fully facing up to the magnitude of the horrors in which they were so grievously complicit and making reparations.

16. https://www.slavevoyages.org/assessment/estimates

17. Martin Meredith, 2016, *The Fortunes of Africa: A 5000- Year History of Wealth, Greed and Endeavour,* New York: PublicAffairs.

18. https://www.slavevoyages.org/assessment/estimates

19. https://www.independent.co.uk/news/uk/home-news/britain-s-colonial-shame-slaveownersgiven-huge-payouts-after-abolition-8508358.html?r=389

20. Nick Draper, 2007, 'Possessing Slaves: Ownership, Compensation and Metropolitan Society at the time of Emancipation 1834-40', History Workshop Journal, Volume 64, Issue 1, pp 74-102, pp. 96.

21. https://www.ucl.ac.uk/lbs/project/catherine/

22. Nick Draper, op. cit.

23. https://www.nationalarchives.gov.uk/pathways/blackhistory/rights/docs/state_trials.htm

24. https://equiano.uk/

25. https://www.oxforddnb.com/view/10.1093/ref:odnb/9780198614128.001.0001/odnb-9780198614128-e-92867

26. https://web.archive.org/web/20090311010318/http://www.spartacus.schoolnet.co.uk/REwedgwood.htm

27. Matthew Mason, 2009, 'Keeping up Appearances: The International Politics of Slave Trade Abolition in the Nineteenth-Century Atlantic World', *The William and Mary Quarterly*, Third Series, Vol. 66, No. 4, 809-832.

28. https://api.parliament.uk/historic-hansard/lords/1807/feb/05/slave-trade-abolition-bill

29. https://www.encyclopedia.com/history/encyclopedias-almanacs-transcripts-and-maps/us-congress-act-prohibit-importation-slaves

30. https://www.encyclopedia.com/history/encyclopedias-almanacs-transcripts-and-maps/us-congress-act-prohibit-importation-slaves

31. https://www.thoughtco.com/international-slave-trade-outlawed-1773975

32. https://db0nus869y26v.cloudfront.net/en/Committee_for_the_Relief_of_the_Black_Poor

33. 'London', London Chronicle 16 January 1787, p2. Cited in Michael Siwa, 2021, 'Why did the Black Poor of London not support the Sierra Leone Resettlement Scheme?' *History Matters* Vol. 1, No. 2, pp25-47.

34. https://en.wikipedia.org/wiki/History_of_Sierra_Leone#The_Province_of_Freedom_(1787%E2%80%9317 89)

35. https://www.williamgladstone.org.uk/slavery

36. https://www.theguardian.com/politics/2006/nov/26/race.immigrationpolicy

37. https://api.parliament.uk/historic-hansard/commons/1823/may/15/

abolition-of-slavery

38.https://en.wikipedia.org/wiki/Slavery_Abolition_Act_1833

39. https://www.pdavis.nl/index.htm

40. Thomas Fowell Buxton, 1839, *The African Slave Trade and Its Remedy*, John Murray, London, p235. https://archive.org/details/africanslavetrad00buxt/page/582/mode/2up

41. J.D.Y. Peel, 2000, *Religious Encounter and the Making of the Yoruba*, Indiana University Press, Bloomington.

42.https://www.europenowjournal.org/2020/10/11/the-burden-of-freedom-therapeutic-architecture-as-self-fashioning-in-the-british-protectorate-of-lagos-1830s-1900/

43. https://www.fao.org/3/a0154e/A0154E05.htm

44. http://www.ampltd.co.uk/collections_az/CMS-4-03/description.aspx

45. http://slaveryandremembrance.org/people/person/?id=PP010

46. Funso Aiyejina, 2009, 'Esu Elegbara: A Source of an Alter/Native Theory of African Literature and Criticism' https://sta.uwi.edu/newspics/2009/Esu%20Elegbara3.pdf

47. T. J. Bowen, 1857, Adventures and Missionary Labours in Several Countries in the Interior of Africa from 1849 to 1856, Southern Baptist Publication Society, Charleston, p142 https://archive.org/details/centralafricaadv00bowe_0

48. Samuel Crowther, Journals 29/7/1853, CMS CA2/O/31.

49. Bowen, p166. https://theculturetrip.com/africa/benin/articles/meet-the-dahomey-amazons-the-all-female-warriors-of-west-africa/

50. Bowen, p139.

51. Bowen, p296-297.

52. http://slaveryandremembrance.org/articles/article/?id=A0121

53. CMS, CA2061/SO, King, 17th Aug 1853, cited by Francine Shields, 1997, Palm Oil and Power; Women in an Era of Economic and Social Transition in 19th Century Yorubaland, PhD Thesis, University of Sterling, p21.

54.https://www.blackpast.org/global-african-history/tinubu-madam-efunroye-ca-1805-1887/

55. Bowen, pp.304-5.

56. Bowen, pp.304-5.

Printed in Great Britain
by Amazon

12578454R00142